THE GREAT BOOK OF CRAZY PRESIDENT TRIVIA

Interesting Stories of American Presidents

American History & Trivia

By

Bill O'Neill

&

Dwayne Walker

ISBN-13: 978-1977912138

CONTENTS

INTRODUCTION

Do you find yourself interested in politics? Do you want to learn all of the fun facts and interesting stories about the current president as well as the presidents of the past? If so, then this book is exactly what you are looking for. In this book, not only are you going to learn about important events that happened during each of the presidencies, but you will learn all about the presidents, their quirks, and personal lives.

You will see how they are just like the rest of us, although sometimes even weirder. You will learn how the heroes of this nation led in times that were filled with strife and how they behaved in public and in private. Some of them were hilarious, some odd, and some of them were just plain mean.

Looking back and learning about the presidents of the past, you cannot help but relate to the events that happened in their time because they are so much like what we are facing today.

You will learn all about your favorite presidents, the forgotten presidents, and even those that you are not fond of, but there is one thing that will remain true. No matter what your opinion of them, they did serve or are serving as the President of the United States, and for that they deserve all of our respect.

CHAPTER ONE

RUMOR, MYTH, OR THE TRUTH

There are many stories that are told about our former and present presidents. However, many people are not able to tell the difference between the rumors, myths, and the truth when it comes to the leaders of the free world. Many of the stories that people believe are myths turn out to be true, and many of the stories that people believe to be true are merely myths.

Are you able to tell the difference? The truth is that these men who have been charged with running the entire United States of America, while they have been built up to be more over the years, they are merely human. It can be very surprising to learn the truth about these men.

President George Washington

Did the first president of the United States grow marijuana on his plantation? This is a very common belief. The fact is that George Washington did grow hemp on his plantation, harvesting it for industrial purposes. The hemp that George

Washington grew was used for making thread which was used in clothing, as well as rope, sail canvases, and fishing nets.

In the 1760s, George Washington thought that hemp could be more profitable than tobacco. He even wrote to England in order to determine how much it would cost to produce and ship the crop. However, later he decided that wheat was the better option. George Washington continued to grow hemp, however, but only enough to use on his own plantation.

Hemp is also known as *Cannabis sativa,* however, this is not the same thing as *Cannabis sativa indicia* or marijuana. The hemp that George Washington grew on his plantation contained less than 0.3 percent THC. This means that it would have had no effect on the body or the mind. Therefore, it could not have been used as a drug. The marijuana that is sold today contains up to 20 percent THC.

This means that the story of George Washington growing marijuana is not true. However, it is true that the first president of the United States of America grew hemp on his plantation.

George Washington's Teeth

George Washington sent out a message on the 29th of May in 1781 that was intercepted by the British. They wondered what the message might contain—information about a spy, or maybe information about the Army? When they opened it, much to their surprise it had nothing to do with the new nation but instead was about George Washington's teeth.

The letter was supposed to reach Dr. John Baker, who was one of George Washington's dentists. This was not the only correspondence that Washington had sent in regard to his teeth. In fact, the president at the time had suffered due to his teeth for the majority of his life. The abscesses, decay, and other oral issues had not only caused General Washington a huge amount of pain, but they had caused him a large amount of embarrassment as well.

George Washington had his first tooth pulled at only 24 years of age, even though he had tried very hard to take care of his teeth.

It was no secret that George Washington suffered greatly due to his teeth. John Adams stated that Washington believed his oral problems were due to cracking walnuts with his teeth when he was a child.

Washington had even gone as far as summoning a French dentist by the name of Jean Pierre Le Mayeur to New York during the Revolutionary War to provide dental care. By the time that Washington was 47, he was wearing false teeth that had been wired around the few natural teeth that remained in his mouth.

Even in the 1700s the President of the US was concerned

about the way he looked, stating that his current dentures made his lips bulge out so much that they looked very swollen. In 1797, he ordered what would be his last set of dentures.

While George Washington was President of the US, he had only one tooth remaining in his mouth which was also lost eventually. However, the President cared so much about his oral health that he carried around a dental set which contained toothpaste (called tooth powder at the time), a toothbrush, a tongue scraper, and even dental cleaning tools which are very similar to what we see in the dentist's office today.

It has been said over the years that George Washington had a set of wooden dentures, however, this simply is not true. It is possible that his dentures looked as if they were made of wood because of staining, but wood has never been used to create dentures. During his lifetime, George Washington had many sets of dentures, both full and partial. Some of them were made out of human teeth and some of cow and horse teeth, ivory, brass, copper, and silver, but none of them were made out of wood.

The human teeth that were used in George Washington's dentures came from two sources. Washington had kept some of his teeth that had been pulled in a locked desk drawer. Nine of the teeth came from African-Americans. It was found in one of George Washington's account books that he paid

122 shillings for nine teeth from "negroes." While this may seem disgusting by our standards today, in the 1700s, it was common for affluent people to purchase teeth from others to be used in their dentures.

President John Adams

President John Adams married Abigail Adams when he was 29 years old and she was 20. They had met five years prior, but it was not love at first sight. John had visited the Smith home because his friend Richard was interested in courting Abigail's sister, Mary.

John was not impressed upon the first visit, describing the three Smith girls as not frank, not fond, and not candid. He wrote that Abigail's mother had not thought much of him and that he was lacking manners.

However, his mind would soon be changed as he continued to visit the family while Richard courted Mary and while he attended to business in Weymouth. John Adams and Abigail Smith were married on the 25th of October in 1764.

The two would have to endure many separations during their marriage. However, they wrote thousands of letters to each other during these times. Of the letters that the two wrote back and forth, 1160 of them survived. Reading through those letters we are able to learn how much the two actually loved each other.

Abigail and John were the first to live in the White House. It was still under construction at that point, and Abigail was known for hanging her laundry out to dry in what was known as the East Room.

The Boston Massacre

It was March 5th in 1770 when the Redcoat, Private Hugh White, suffered an assault by a crowd of boys. Snowballs were thrown, along with stones, clubs, and oysters that were still in their shells. The Redcoats had been at odds with those who lived in Boston since they had first arrived, and it was inevitable that the tensions would boil over.

Captain Thomas Preston, as well as several soldiers, arrived to protect Private Hugh White, forming a half-circle around him in order to stop the assault and to maintain peace. However, a club was thrown and hit one of the soldiers on his head. The soldier lost his balance, and his musket discharged. This caused the other soldiers to believe that they had been given the order to fire, and weapons were discharged into the crowd. Five civilians were killed that day.

The following day, there was a knock on John Adams' door. It was requested that he defend Captain Preston as well as the rest of the soldiers because no one else would. John Adams did not hesitate to take the case and defend the men. He believed in the law as well as protecting the innocent. He believed that the soldiers had been wrongfully accused and that they had only fired in self-defense.

In the following months, Samuel Adams, the cousin of John Adams would do everything he could to make it seem as if the soldiers were the ones that had started the trouble to begin with. Paul Revere even altered an engraving that had been done by Henry Pelham in order to commemorate the massacre, making it look as if Preston was giving his man the order to shoot.

John Adams argued that the soldiers had no intention of firing into the crowd and that instead they had been the victims and had fired due to duress. Preston was found not guilty, thanks to John Adams. Six of the soldiers were found to be innocent, while two of them were convicted of manslaughter. The two that were convicted of manslaughter were not sentenced to prison. Instead, a mark was put upon their thumbs and they were let free.

John Adams wanted to prove that everyone had the right to a fair trial in the United States and make sure that the innocent did not receive punishment. He wanted to make sure that even the Redcoats were represented in the court of law and that the law was upheld. Later, John Adams would describe the trial as one of the best pieces of service that he had ever rendered his country.

"I pray Heaven to bestow the best of blessings on this House and all that shall hereafter inhabit it. May none but honest and wise men ever rule under this roof." – John Adams

President Thomas Jefferson

The third President of the United States was the father of several children by Sally Hemings, his slave concubine… Or was he?

Back during President Jefferson's first term, it was said that he and Sally Hemings, one of his slaves, had an affair which resulted in the birth of six children. This subject has been debated since Jefferson was in office, however, according to not just oral history but documentation and scientific evidence, it is believed that six years after Jefferson's wife died, he did father six children, and the mother was his slave.

It was against Jefferson's policy to respond to public attacks. Therefore, he did not respond to the accusations at the time they were made. His children later denied that it was possible for him to have fathered other children by Sally Hemings. However, DNA evidence proved that Eston Hemings, the youngest child of Sally Hemings carried the Jefferson Y chromosome. These DNA results were released in late 1998, and later the Thomas Jefferson Foundation stated that there was a high probability that Jefferson was the father of not just one of Sally Heming's children but all six of them.

According to the accounts of Sally's mother, Sally was Thomas Jefferson's father-in-law's daughter, or the half-sister of his late wife.

Jefferson on Dogs

We all know that it is said that a dog is a man's best friend. If you were to have asked Thomas Jefferson his opinion on this saying, he may have agreed with you, but then again, he may not have. It would have depended on when you asked him.

In 1789, Thomas Jefferson liked dogs. He liked shepherd's dogs the most, believing that they were the original breed of dogs. We do not know exactly what these dogs looked like, but what we do know is that Jefferson was willing to go to extreme lengths to obtain one.

Jefferson visited France, walking for miles through wind and rain trying to find one of these dogs. To Jefferson, the dog was worth all the trouble because he believed that they were the most intelligent breed of dogs.

Jefferson was finally able to purchase a dog, whose name was Bergere. She was pregnant when he took her back to Virginia, which was perfect because he had planned on bringing many of the animals from Europe to the New World. Thomas Jefferson was very proud of Bergere and her pups, stating that they knew how to herd every animal, even chickens.

Word of the dogs spread quickly, and soon Jefferson was receiving letters from friends asking if they could have one of the shepherd's dogs as well. Jefferson purchased another shepherd's dog and named him Grizzle, but later his opinion of dogs changed, and he decided that the dog's pups were too much trouble and had them all killed. He even had all of the dogs of his slaves killed, stating that he did not want them eating the sheep.

As Thomas Jefferson grew older, his opinion of dogs continued to decline. He was very hostile toward dogs, stating that they were an affliction to men and that he would readily take part in exterminating the entire species.

President James Madison

Homeschooling is still seen as controversial, even in the age in which we live. There are those who wonder if it is possible for a child who is educated at home to become successful later in life. James Madison, the fourth President of the United States, known to be the chief architect of the Constitution of the United States, is proof that it is possible.

Madison was so intelligent that he completed his undergraduate degree at Princeton in just two years, which made him the very first Princeton graduate student.

It is doubtful that without James Madison the Constitution would have been accepted as the law, and it is quite possible that the Articles of the Confederation would have been adopted instead.

James Madison led our nation during the War of 1812 when the British seized D.C. and burnt the White House as well as the Capitol Building.

When the White House caught on fire, it was not James Madison who was the hero. Instead, it was his wife, Dolly. James Madison ran in fear from the White House while Dolly stayed behind and saved a portrait of George Washington, which took some doing. You see, the portrait was securely attached to the wall. Dolly had a few of the slaves help her with the portrait and stated that she stayed until it was safe.

While James Madison might not have been the most courageous president, he was a very intelligent one, and without him the nation would not be what it is today.

President James Monroe

Born in Westmoreland, Virginia, on the 28th of April in 1758, James Monroe started attending the University of William and Mary at the young age of 16. He fought in the Revolutionary War, in which he was injured. When he was 28, he married Elizabeth Kortright, who was 17 at the time.

James Monroe is the first United States president to not wear knee breeches. Instead, he wore long pants. He was also the first US Senator to be elected to the position of US President. James Monroe was elected while the White House was being rebuilt, and it was the year that he became president that it was painted white.

In 1820, he ran for his second term unopposed and received all but four of the electoral votes. It is rumored that John Quincy Adams received one vote and three electors did not vote. Monroe was the only president other than George Washington to ever receive a unanimous vote. The only reason that the delegate in New Hampshire voted for Adams was because he wanted to make sure that George Washington was the only president to receive a unanimous vote.

Thanks to President Monroe, Missouri and Maine became states. After serving in public office for over 40 years, President Monroe was poor and had to live with his daughter for a year before he died on the 4th of July 1831.

President John Quincy Adams

We hear of people claiming corruption all the time, but imagine what would happen if during an election no candidate received enough electoral votes to become president, but instead, the House of Representatives chose the president.

That is exactly what happened in 1824. There were five candidates in the election of 1824— John C. Calhoun, Henry Clay, William H. Crawford, Andrew Jackson, and John

Quincy Adams. Jackson was actually ahead in the votes, both popular and electoral, however, no one candidate received enough electoral votes to be elected.

The election was then turned over to the House of Representatives. Clay, the Speaker of the House, supported Adams, and it was Adams who became President of the US. Later, Clay would be Adams' Secretary of State. This, of course, enraged Jackson and his supporters. Jackson, at that time, was serving on the Senate. However, he resigned. In 1828, he ran for President of the US once again, and this time he was successful.

John Quincy Adams faced hostility from those who supported Jackson, which resulted in him being blocked from making any real progress. This was much like what we see going on today. His proposal of a federally funded road system, a national university, and providing territory to the Native Americans failed, as he received no support from Congress.

President Andrew Jackson

Finally, in 1828 Andrew Jackson experienced victory and won the presidency. However, in 1835, Richard Lawrence attempted to assassinate the President, making him the first president to ever experience an attempt of assassination.

Richard Lawrence, a house painter who was unemployed at

the time, approached the president as he left a funeral and attempted to shoot him. However, Lawrence's gun misfired. Jackson was furious and attacked Lawrence, beating him with his cane. Lawrence pulled out a second gun and pointed it at the president, but this gun also misfired. Jackson was pulled off of Lawrence by his aides and was unharmed, although the experience left him very paranoid.

It is likely that Lawrence was suffering from some mental instability. However, the president believed that the man had been hired by the Democrats and the Whig Party to assassinate him. Jackson believed this because at the time he was trying to pull the Bank of the United States apart. Martin Van Buren, who was Jackson's vice president, also became very paranoid and began to carry two pistols with him whenever he visited the Senate.

Later, the Smithsonian Institute tested both of Lawrence's guns, and they both fired without any problem. The odds of both of the guns misfiring when he was trying to assassinate the president were 1 in 125,000.

A Tragic Love Story

Andrew Jackson met Rachel, his wife, in Nashville, Tennessee. He had been orphaned by the age of 14, which led to him being quite wild due to a lack of parental influence. Jackson gambled, visited brothels, and lost a lot of money, but he continued to carry on. He ended up studying law because he wanted to make something of his life, and then he headed West because he knew there were opportunities there. That was when he met Rachel.

The relationship, however, was very controversial, because when Jackson met Rachel, she was already married to another man. The man Rachel was married to was abusive, and he was always accusing her of flirting with other men or having affairs. At that time, divorce was not as acceptable as it is now, and it was quite difficult to get a divorce approved. Rachel's husband did end up filing for divorce, but it took a long time. It was during this time that Rachel and Jackson eloped.

When they arrived back in Nashville, Rachel's family accepted Jackson, as did her family and her friends. When the divorce finally came through, her first husband charged Rachel with adultery.

Rachel was at the center of Jackson's life. She brought peace into his life, gave him love, and made him very happy. The relationship between Jackson and Rachel was very stable and, surprisingly, it was not affected when he became a public figure.

Andrew Jackson became very famous during the war of 1812 after the Battle of New Orleans. Jackson was a hero, and people began to say that he would make a good candidate for president. During this time, his feelings never changed for her. He was never ashamed of her or her past. People referred to her as a little fat dumpling because she was short and fat. She had a country accent, and she was not well-educated, but Jackson thought that Rachel was perfect.

During the 1828 election, some enemies of Jackson had learned that there was something off about the marriage. They searched the public records and found that Rachel had been divorced due to adultery, and the newspapers began a smear campaign. Rachel was called a bigamist as well as an adulteress, and it was written that she should not be allowed into the White House, let alone be in charge. Rachel and Jackson were nearing their 60s at the time, which was quite old for the day. The two had lived their lives as respectable people, and Rachel took the smear campaign quite hard, which infuriated Jackson.

Rachel was the first wife of any candidate to be attacked by the newspapers. Of course, we know that she would not be the last that the media would attack. Today, presidential candidates' wives know that the media consider them fair game.

Just after the election, before the couple could ever move into the White House, Rachel suffered a heart attack and died. Jackson believed that it was due to those who had ruined her reputation, and he swore he would never forgive them.

Jackson was a mess his entire first term because he missed Rachel so much, and not a lot of time was spent on national business.

Their story was special because it is a true American love story. They did not care what anyone thought of their relationship, and they did not care that divorce was unacceptable when they were married. They just loved each other for their entire lives.

President Martin Van Buren

The first president of the United States to be born in the United States, Van Buren started his time in office facing an economic depression. Van Buren had inherited the downturn in the economy which began in 1836. It was the main focus of his presidency.

There were three main causes of the depression. The first was that the English banks, in response to financial issues in England, had stopped pumping money into America. This money had funded the entire economy as well as growth for two decades.

The second reason was because the US banks had given too much credit, and when the British banks stopped providing the US with money, the banks started calling the loans in. The third reason was Jackson's money policies. Jackson forced all federal land purchases to be made with precious metals instead of paper money, which caused more credit problems.

The demand for US cotton plummeted, which caused prices to drop by 50 percent. Those in the South suffered, as well as the northern companies, due to the drop in the price of cotton. In April 1837, prices around the entire world collapsed. By May 10th, all of the banks in New York stopped trading paper money for silver and gold. Banks in many other cities, such as New Orleans, did the same.

This caused panic throughout the nation, which in turn caused banks to fail. Many believed that this would be the end of the United States. By the beginning of 1838, a half-million Americans were unemployed.

The economy soon rebounded briefly. However, by October 1839, there was a second panic which caused another four years of depression.

Of course, people blamed Van Buren for the depression. The Whigs claimed that it was Jackson's policies, which Van Buren had carried forward, that caused the crisis. They claimed that all the nation needed was stabilization of the economy by a government-sponsored national bank.

Van Buren believed that it was the greedy American businesses and banks that were the cause of the economic collapse. He proposed creating an independent US treasury. Doing this would ensure that the nation's money supply would not be affected by politics. This treasury was going to ensure that the funds were kept in gold as well as silver, which would ensure that money was not printed at will but instead that it was covered by the gold and silver the nation had in the treasury. This was also supposed to prevent any inflation.

This was proposed in 1837; however, it took three years before it would be accepted by the Democrats and Whigs. It was Van Buren who set up our national treasury as it is today.

Removal of the Cherokee

It was also Van Buren who directed that all Cherokee who had not complied with the Treaty of New Echota be forcibly removed. The Cherokee were supposed to leave all the Southeastern states and move into what is today Oklahoma.

Those who had not left the Southeastern states were taken to internment camps where they were kept for the entire summer of 1838. They were to be transported west, however, this was delayed until the fall due to the drought and intense heat during the summer months. When fall arrived, the Cherokee agreed that they would take themselves west. Twenty-thousand Cherokee traveled the Trail of Tears in the relocation.

President William Henry Harrison

William Henry Harrison ran for president in 1836 and lost. However, when he ran again in 1840, he won, receiving 80 percent of the electoral votes. Harrison's campaign was the first to use advertising as well as slogans.

William Henry Harrison would have the shortest presidency ever though his inaugural address was the longest ever. He spoke even though it was freezing cold outside. He was caught in the rain, and then as it began to get colder, he finally ended the speech. This resulted in his becoming very ill, which would result in his death just one month after he took office.

Many believe that the death of William Henry Harrison was the result of Tecumseh's Curse. The Curse of Tippecanoe, or Tecumseh's Curse, is the belief that every president elected in a year that ends with zero dies in office.

It is believed that Tecumseh, who was a Native American leader, cursed William Henry Harrison. Tecumseh was a Shawnee who traveled among many tribes, bringing them together to fight against the white people.

William Henry Harrison was the governor of the Indian Territory at that time and was to confront Tecumseh and his warriors. Harrison organized a group that consisted of one thousand men in November 1811. The group gathered outside of Prophetstown, which Tecumseh had founded.

Tecumseh was gone, recruiting other Indians to join him in his cause, however, his brother Tenskwatawa was in

Prophetstown and ordered an attack. The Native Americans were defeated, and Tecumseh's Confederacy dissolved. This became known as the Battle of Tippecanoe, and later Harrison would use it in his slogan for the presidency, "Tippecanoe and Tyler too."

During the war of 1812, Tecumseh sided with the British. Killed by a gunshot on October 1813, Tecumseh's body was mutilated, and he was later buried in a mass grave. After Tecumseh was killed, the Indian Confederacy dissolved completely, and there was no way to stop settlers from moving into what would later become Ohio.

From Harrison up to Ronald Regan, every president that was elected in a year that ended in zero died while in office.

Harrison was elected in 1840 and died in office due to pneumonia.

Lincoln was elected in 1860 and was assassinated.

Garfield was elected in 1880 and was assassinated.

McKinley was elected in 1900 and was assassinated.

Harding was elected in 1920 and died from pneumonia.

Roosevelt was elected in 1940 and died from a cerebral hemorrhage.

JFK was elected in 1960 and was assassinated.

Ronald Regan was elected in 1980, and while he was shot in the chest, he lived, causing many to wonder if this was the end of the curse.

George W. Bush was elected in 2000 and lived, proving that the curse was broken.

Not only was it believed that the president had to be elected in a year that ended with zero, but that it was to happen every 20 years. However, Taylor died in 1850 due to drinking bad water or milk, or eating bad cherries. No one really knows for sure what it was that killed him. There were also three presidents who were not elected in zero years who experienced assassination attempts; however, they lived. Therefore, many wonder if the curse ever really existed.

Was there really a curse, and if there was, is it really over? There is no way for us to ever know if Tecumseh put a curse on Harrison or any of the presidents; however, the belief in the curse is not something that is going to be going away anytime soon.

President John Tyler

John Tyler was the first president to not be elected president, causing many to refer to him as an accidental president. His wife died while he was in office, and he was the first president to get married while he was in office. No other president had more children than Tyler, who had 15.

Tyler joined the Confederacy shortly after Lincoln was elected, and he himself was elected to the Confederate House of Representatives. However, he died before taking his seat.

During the war, the Union destroyed Tyler's summer home. They later destroyed his plantation, Sherwood Forest, breaking and burning most of his possessions. People considered John Tyler a traitor because he joined the Confederacy.

He died in a hotel in Richmond, a sworn enemy of the United States. At the time, Tyler was 71 years old, and just 18 months earlier, his youngest child had been born.

When he died, there was no recognition given because he was considered a traitor. However, it would be Jimmy Carter who would restore Tyler's citizenship over 100 years later.

RANDOM FUN FACTS

1. John Adams is one of only three United States Presidents to not attend the inauguration of his successor.
2. John Adams was known for skipping school when he was a young boy, wanting to spend his time fishing and hunting instead of learning.
3. Thomas Jefferson founded the University of Virginia in 1819, on land that once belonged to James Monroe. He was the only president to ever fund a university.
4. Tyler greatly opposed the Missouri Compromise, believing that the federal government restricting slavery should be illegal. He believed in the rights of the states as well as the rights of the people. He also believed that government should be limited and that it should stay out of the business of the people.
5. Tyler's wife Julia had a premonition about his death. She was supposed to meet him a few days later, but after dreaming of his death immediately went to him. He died just over one week later.
6. George Washington distributed liquor that was made in his distillery in Mount Vernon. He made apple brandy, peach brandy, and rye whiskey.

7. Thomas Jefferson and John Adams were very close friends, however, they were also rivals. They had what we would describe today as a love-hate relationship. On the 4th of July 1826, while Adams was dying, he whispered, "Thomas Jefferson survives," however, Jefferson had actually died just a few hours before.

8. Adams and Jefferson were both fans of Shakespeare, and together they visited his home in 1786 where the two vandalized Shakespeare's chair, chipping a piece off of it to keep for a souvenir. How is that for presidential behavior?

9. James Madison is referred to as the Father of the Constitution. James Madison spent hours studying governments from all over the world before coming up with the ideas that the Constitution was based on. Of course, he did not write the Constitution on his own, but it was Madison who made sure there was population-based representation, and he ensured that we had a strong checks and balances system.

10. John Quincy Adams loved to go skinny-dipping in the early mornings in the Potomac River while he served as president. Imagine the social media posts and news stories we would see today if our president skinny-dipped in the river.

11. Andrew Jackson was a man of many duels. He took part

in at least 100 duels over the years, most of them to defend Rachel's honor. Jackson was even shot in the chest in 1806 in a duel. Thomas Hart Benton, a Missouri senator, also shot Jackson in the arm when the two got into a fight in a bar.

12. Van Buren popularized the term O.K. He was nicknamed Old Kinderhook due to the fact that he grew up in Kinderhook, New York. The term O.K. Clubs sprang up during his campaign, and later O.K. was used to state that one was all right.

13. During Harrison's campaign, the Democrats tried to smear him, stating that he was out of touch and that he would rather sip his hard cider while sitting in his log cabin than he would run the country. Harrison, however, was a smart man and used their smear campaign against them. He used the log cabin and the hard cider in his own campaign, even having bottles of cider made that were in the shape of log cabins.

14. Lyon Tyler, the grandson of President Tyler, is still alive at the time of this writing. Thirty-five presidents after his grandfather held office, Lyon Tyler has seen the United States change in many ways, but in other ways it has remained the same. When we look back at the stories of the times of our former presidents, we can see that the same thing is going on in our nation as we speak.

15. Thomas Jefferson had an entire set of mastodon bones from 40 million years prior sent to the White House, and he tried to assemble them in what we now know as the East Room. Who knew he wanted to be an archaeologist?

TEST YOURSELF- QUESTIONS AND ANSWERS

1. Who was the minister to France who helped to negotiate the Louisiana Purchase? This man was the President from 1817 to 1825.

   A. William Henry Harrison

   B. Andrew Jackson

   C. James Monroe

2. Who was the son of a former president who began the program to build canals and highways?

   A. John Tyler

   B. Thomas Jefferson

   C. John Quincy Adams

3. Who was born in 1790, attended the William and Mary College, and was also the first vice president to succeed?

   A. Martin Van Buren

   B. John Tyler

   C. James Monroe

4. Who drafted the Declaration of Independence when he was 33 years of age and became the President of the United States from 1801 to 1809?

A. George Washington
B. Andrew Jackson
C. Thomas Jefferson

5. Who was born in Massachusetts in 1735, served as vice president twice, and then was President of the United States from 1797 to 1801?

A. William Henry Harrison
B. John Adams
C. John Quincy Adams

ANSWERS

1. C
2. C
3. B
4. C
5. B

CHAPTER TWO
IT WAS A DIFFERENT WORLD

When you read about the early years of the United States, it is obvious that it was a completely different world. Strange was the world that they lived in when it took two years to graduate from an Ivy League University, when a gambler that visited burlesque houses regularly could ascend to be the leader of the free world, and where something as simple as getting too cold could cause the end of one's life. The truth is, however, that we have not come as far as we would like to think. We still have the same problems that many presidents of the past faced—economic problems, unemployment, smear campaigns, Congress blocking all attempts of the president, and so on. It may have been a different time, but it was not an easier one, as many would like to believe. Let's check out some interesting stories about our next ten presidents and discover how the times began to change.

President James K. Polk

James K. Polk was not the most interesting of presidents,

however, at the time he was elected, he was the youngest president to have been elected. Growing up, Polk was what one would call a weakling. At 17, he had to have kidney stones surgically removed without the use of anesthesia or any antiseptics. It is believed that this surgery left Polk sterile because he never fathered any children.

Polk was homeschooled due to his health problems. However, after he recovered from surgery, his father offered to introduce him into the mercantile business, but Polk was not interested. Instead, he enrolled in the Zion Church and just one year later the academy in Murfreesboro.

It was in Murfreesboro that he met Sarah Childress, who would later become his wife. In 1816, he began attending the University of North Carolina, which at the time had no more than 80 students enrolled.

While attending school, he joined the Dialectic Society, where he learned how to debate. In 1818, Polk graduated from the University of North Carolina with honors. Next, he would travel to Nashville where he would study law. On the 29th of September 1819, Polk was elected clerk of the Tennessee State Senate. He was re-elected in 1821, unopposed, as well as in 1822.

In 1820, he took the bar. His first client was his father, who was charged with fighting in public. Polk was able to secure his father's release, and his father had to pay one dollar in fines. His law practice was very successful, mostly because there were so many cases during the Panic of 1819.

In 1822, he joined the militia and was appointed to the position of colonel by Governor William Carroll. He earned the nickname Napoleon of the Stump. In 1823, he ran for state legislature and became the representative of Maury County. He was friends with Andrew Jackson in 1823 and voted for him to become the next Tennessee Senator. The two become strong friends afterward.

Finally, in 1824, at the age of 24, he married Sarah Childress. Sarah was 20. Sarah was an asset to Polk's political career, drafting his speeches and providing him with advice when it came to policy. She was also very active in his campaigns.

In 1826, Polk made a speech about how the electoral college should be eliminated and stated that presidents should be elected by popular vote. He was a vocal critic of Adams and often voted against any policy that he put forth.

While he was president, he oversaw the founding of the US Naval Academy, the creation of the first postage stamp, and the beginning of the Washington Monument. Over 800,000 square miles were added to the US during his presidency, which extended the borders all the way to the Pacific Ocean.

He was a devout Methodist who had never had a drink, had

never danced, nor did he have much of a personality. The Polks were so devout that no music or dancing was allowed at James Polk's inaugural ball from the time that the family arrived until the time that they left.

Just one week before he died, Polk snuck a baptism in. He had contracted cholera while traveling outside of the US; however, the official cause of death was listed as diarrhea.

While Polk is considered one of the forgotten presidents, he was one of the most successful of them. He was also the first president to retire voluntarily after serving only one term.

President Zachary Taylor

Nicknamed Old Rough and Ready, Taylor was the 12th president of the United States of America and died on the 9th of July 1850. The official cause of death was due to spending too much time in the sun and then eating cherries, cucumbers, and iced milk.

It is stated that on the 4th of July in 1850, Taylor became overheated while he was out in the July sun. In order to cool himself off, he ate several cucumbers, a bowl of cherries, and then drank a pitcher of milk. Five days later he was dead.

Some believe that Taylor was poisoned, and believe it or not, the evidence that points to arsenic poisoning is quite strong. The rumors of his poisoning spread very quickly; however, there were other rumors as well. Some said that he had died from food poisoning, cholera, and typhoid fever.

However, there was always the theory that he was assassinated by poison. In 1991, Professor Clara Rising convinced descendants of Taylor to allow his body to be exhumed. The coffin was taken out of the ground, and it was found that his remains were in very good shape.

Studies showed that his tissue contained high levels of arsenic. However, it was decided that the levels were not high enough to prove poisoning. This did not put an end to the rumor. According to Michael Parenti, who wrote *History as Mystery*, there were several mistakes made during the autopsy and the findings had been flawed.

According to Parenti, the amount of arsenic that was found in Taylor's hair was roughly the same as other victims of arsenic poisoning. Antimony had also been found in the hair, which is another poison.

Why would someone want to assassinate Taylor? That is the question that many people find themselves asking. Many believe it could have been due to slavery. Taylor was a slave owner; however, when it came to the issue of slavery, he was considered a moderate. Taylor did not support the Compromise of 1850, which stated that all runaway slaves were to be returned to their owners. Henry Clay, who was the author of the bill, attacked Taylor in the Senate.

States were threatening secession, and Taylor responded with threats of military action against those that threatened secession, stating that they were traitors. It seemed certain that civil war was on the horizon. However, it was the death of Taylor that brought peace temporarily. It also allowed Fillmore to take office. Fillmore was a supporter of the Compromise of 1850.

Today, we may not think of Taylor as a very important president. However, if it was not for that 4th of July, we may have been remembering him as the president during the Civil War instead of Abraham Lincoln.

The theory that he was assassinated is credible. Many pro-slavery advocates, some of them very powerful, had motive to kill the president. If this case is revisited by historical detectives, they may just find that it was Taylor who was the first president to die at the hands of an assassin instead of Lincoln.

President Millard Fillmore

Millard Fillmore rode the coattails of Taylor into office because Taylor had died just over a year after he had taken office. Fillmore had been born in central New York in a log cabin. He was part of the Whig Party. As vice president, he was mostly ignored; however, he did get Taylor's attention when he stated that he was going to support the Compromise of 1850, which stood for everything that Tylor was opposed to.

When Taylor died, Fillmore became even more of a supporter of the Compromise of 1850. While he may have postponed the Civil War, the peace that he brought came with a price.

The Compromise was supposed to end the conflict between those who were for slavery and those who were against, however, neither side was satisfied. Fillmore did not help because he was against slavery. However, he did not act on those beliefs but instead enforced the Fugitive Slave Act of 1850, which targeted not only slaves who had escaped but also African-Americans who were free.

By the time Fillmore had served his three years as President, the members of the Whig party were very mad at him, and he was not nominated to represent their party in the next election. The chosen candidate for the Whig party was not successful, which made Fillmore the last president to represent the Whig party.

By the time Fillmore's presidency was coming to an end, he was facing difficulties in his personal life. Abigail, his wife, had become ill on the very day that he had been sworn in. Abigail had died within one month of Fillmore taking office, and it was not long after that his daughter died as well.

In order to deal with the loss of his family, he tried to remain active in politics. In 1856, he was the presidential candidate for the Know-Nothing Party, a new party. This party was opposed to immigration, and they wanted to put a limit on the number of Irish Catholics allowed into the US.

Fillmore did not agree with this policy. However, he was not able to voice his opinions about it. Out of the three major candidates in that election, Fillmore finished third. After losing the election, Fillmore moved to Buffalo, New York, and retired. He was married a second time to Caroline McIntosh, who was a wealthy widow, and he remained an important figure in Buffalo.

Americans were still divided when it came to the issue of slavery, and while Fillmore's compromise did delay a civil war, it did not stop the Civil War from ever happening.

President Franklin Pierce

There is a list of forgettable presidents that served in the early to mid-19th century, however, Peirce may be the most forgettable. He was president from 1853 to 1857, and while Fillmore is referred to as the least-known president, Pierce is not even known well enough to carry that title.

It is rumored that he hit a woman while driving his carriage drunk. In 1856, he was denied the re-nomination, which made him the only president elected who was not put up for reelection. After this, he told one of his friends that there was nothing left to do but get drunk.

While many, if they were put in the same position, would have been more than happy to stop at the closest bar, it is believed that Pierce was joking when he said it. It was well known that Pierce was a heavy drinker and that it was most likely alcoholism that led to his life ending, however, he did not make announcing his drinking a habit.

The truth is that there is not a single newspaper story about the president at the time of running over a woman with his carriage, which is enough to convince historians that it did not happen. There is absolutely no evidence this ever occurred; however, many still believe to this day that it did.

Pierce also believed in following the Constitution to the letter, and he spoke out against the Civil War. After Lincoln was assassinated, a group gathered in Concord, New Hampshire—which was Pierce's hometown—expressing their grief and confronting those who were not displaying the United States flag after such a tragedy had occurred.

Between 200 and 400 people approached Pierce's home, demanding to know where his flag was. He told them that he did not have to show that he was devoted to the stars and stripes. He told the mob of how his ancestors had participated in the Revolutionary War and the War of 1812, and how he had given 35 years of his life to not only serve New Hampshire but the nation as well.

It is unknown whether or not he swayed the crowd, or if they just tired of listening to him speak. Either way, they did not burn his house down.

Better as an Ex-President

Pierce was much like Jimmy Carter in that he was better at being an ex-president than he was at being a president. After leaving office, he focused on taking care of Jane, his wife, who had tuberculosis and was dying a very slow death. In the winter of 1857, the couple went to Madeira, a Portuguese island. It was there that they studied French, as they were planning on touring Europe.

They traveled Europe from 1858 to 1859, traveling to Switzerland, Italy, Paris, and even London. When they returned to the US, Pierce kept himself busy by buying different properties in New Hampshire. In the winter of 1859, he and Jane traveled to the Bahamas.

Hair, Hair, Hair

Today, we find many people talking about hair, specifically presidential comb-overs. However, Pierce is known as the president that had the perfect comb-over. His head was covered in black curly hair that was combed at an angle over his forehead which was quite wide. It is not just the hair of presidents today that causes discussions, but historians find themselves wrestling with Pierce's hair even to this day.

President James Buchanan

The only president who never married but instead chose to remain a bachelor his whole life, James Buchanan is also considered by many historians to be the worst president of all time. What did he do that made people think he was such a terrible leader?

Today, we know Buchanan for being single throughout his entire life. He was the only president from Pennsylvania, and he was president before Lincoln took office.

It is the Civil War, or his indifference to it, that causes so many academics to label him as the worst president ever. Lincoln, of course, would be a hard president to precede or succeed. Warren Harding, who was scandal-plagued, is usually considered the biggest contender for the title against Buchanan for worst president.

Buchanan served as a member of the House of Representatives five times, he was James Polk's secretary of state, and he served as the US minister to Great Britain. In 1856, Buchannan took the lead at the Democratic convention from Pierce, and then he and Stephen Douglas battled for the nomination.

Buchanan won the nomination and was elected president over John C. Fremont, who represented the Republican Party, which was newly formed.

From that point, it all went downhill. Buchanan became very ill soon after being elected. The illness that he suffered from was spread through the hotel he had stayed in when he was traveling as president-elect.

During his inaugural address, he stated that the issue of slavery was of little importance. He was tipped off as to the decision by the Supreme Court in the Dred Scott vs. Sandford case. It is believed that he may have actually influenced the ruling, as he believed that the states should determine if slavery would be allowed.

The decision on the Dred Scott case angered the Republicans and caused problems between the Democratic and Republican Parties. As the Civil War approached, the economy suffered recession as well.

By early 1860, it was obvious that Buchanan was not going to be put up for re-election. He derailed Douglas' campaign during the Democratic convention, as he wanted to be the nominee that would take on Lincoln.

Because the Democrats were not going to put Buchanan up for re-election, John and Douglas Breckinridge were the only two nominees that they had, which basically ensured that

Lincoln would be elected.

In Buchanan's State of the Union address, Buchanan stated that he believed it was illegal for the South to secede, however, there was nothing that the government could do to stop it. He stated that it was up to the Southern States to be responsible to God for the slavery that took place among them. He stated that the people in the North were not any more responsible to fight or interfere with the South than they were to do so in Brazil or Russia.

He refused to get involved in the crisis because he stated that it was not within the power of the president to restore peace to the states. Because Buchanan did not take any action during this time, the Confederacy was able to organize.

While riding to Lincoln's inauguration, Buchanan told the new president that if he was as happy about taking office as he was about leaving, then Lincoln was a very happy man.

During his presidency, Buchanan was obsessed with what was going on in Cuba as well as the Mormon settlers in Utah. He was the lowest-ranked president in 4 different polls, and in every poll conducted since 1948, he ranked as one of the three worst presidents.

After his term was over, he moved to Pennsylvania, where he lived throughout the Civil War and just before he died in 1868 he stated that history would vindicate his memory.

President Abraham Lincoln

Lincoln was a man who grew up poor, who had no formal education, who had suffered from depression for the majority of his life, who believed in charity, and who not only became the President of the United States but may have been the greatest president of all time.

Abraham was born to Thomas and Nancy Lincoln in 1809. He was the second of three children. Sarah, his sister, was born in 1807. Tommy was born in 1812, and it is believed that he died just three days after he was born.

This, of course, saddened Nancy, however, she had faith that everything in life happened for a reason. This was something that she taught her young son when he was just 7 years old.

Abraham was playing near Knob Creek in Hodgenville, Kentucky, when he fell the water. He almost drowned, but amazingly, he was rescued. It was then that his mother told him that his life had been spared for a reason and he was destined for great things. Little did she know just how great.

The experience affected Abraham profoundly for the rest of his life. While he was not religious like his mother, he did have a strong belief in God, and he believed that the things that were meant to happen would happen no matter what.

Just a year later, the family moved to Indiana and life became even more difficult. At the age of 9, Abraham lost his mother to milk sickness. His father soon realized that he was unable to raise the two children on his own and married Sarah Lincoln.

Abe and his sister Sarah had three step-siblings, as well as their new stepmother, who was quite loving. Abe's father loved to work hard, but he also loved gathering with his friends and telling stories. Abraham did as well, and it is reported that this was the one thing the two had in common.

Thomas felt that education was a waste of time, allowing his children to attend school for just two years. It was during this time that Abe focused on learning to read well. He loved reading about Washington and Jefferson, two men whom Abe admired greatly.

Thomas would criticize his son for reading so much. However, his stepmother could tell that Abraham was a smart boy and helped him to find the books he read.

As a teenager, Abraham was very popular. It was well known that he was skilled with an ax, and people loved to listen to his stories. The men in the area were known for gathering in the fields to debate politics. Thomas would sneak into the group in order to drag Abe out and box his ears for not doing his work.

Of course, Abraham always did his work, and as he grew older, he also grew to dislike Thomas. However, he knew it was his duty to continue to help the family until he turned 21. Abraham worked long days, and many times after he had finished his work, Thomas would hire him out to work on other farms. He would then keep any salary that Abe earned.

About the time that Abraham turned 21 and could leave his father's house, Thomas moved the family to Decatur. Abe agreed to help the family move and to help build the cabin but informed his father that he was not going to stay any longer than that.

Not long after moving to Decatur, Abraham left his father's house and started a life of his own. Abraham moved to New Salem and began working as a store clerk. He also asked Mentor Graham, the local schoolmaster, to tutor him.

His world began to expand as he learned about literature, math, science, and history. As he learned his ambition grew, and he decided that he was going to run for office. In 1832, Lincoln ran for the state legislature for the Whig Party, which favored a strong government. It was at that time that the Blackhawk War began and Lincoln did not hesitate to enlist. His men elected him Captain which was a great honor for him.

After the war, Lincoln returned, but it was too late for him to campaign and the election was lost. At 23, he purchased half of the general store where he had worked. At the same time, he purchased a barrel of books, not knowing what books the barrel contained, for a total of 50 cents. When the books arrived, he found that they were law books.

Lincoln read and studied each of the books, deciding that he was going to become a lawyer. He sold his half of the store back to the original owner, but the owner died before he paid Lincoln. He was left with the store and 1000 dollars in bills that had not been paid.

This was a huge amount of money at the time, but Lincoln visited every single creditor and made a promise that he would repay the debt. This took him 15 years to do, but he kept his promise.

Over the next two years of his life, Abraham worked as the postmaster, a land surveyor, a field worker, and he helped clients by drawing up simple legal agreements. The people of New Salem started calling him Honest Abe.

Abraham's reputation spread, and when he ran for state legislature again, he won the election. During this term, he met a woman by the name of Ann Rutledge. Although Abe and Ann were never engaged, they were romantically involved. This romance would come to an abrupt end when Ann was just 22 years old. She died quickly of typhoid fever.

Nancy, Ann's sister who had been in the house the last time that Abe saw his Ann, said that she could never forget how sad Abe looked when he came out of her room after meeting with her for the last time. He was completely inconsolable after Ann's death. He suffered from depression and doubted that he would ever find happiness, become married, or have a family.

Lincoln was elected to the state legislature for a second term, and it was during this time that he accepted an arranged marriage to Mary Owens. He had met Mary three years prior, but upon seeing her again, he began to have second thoughts.

He stated that he knew Mary was oversized but that she had gotten even bigger. He knew that many called her an old maid, but when he looked at her, he could not help but think of his step-mother. He said that it was not due to her withered features, for there was far too much fat for her skin to wrinkle. It was because of her lack of teeth, her weathered appearance, and that he was not pleased with her in the least.

He did, however, agree to uphold his end of the bargain, and he wrote her a letter stating as much. When he did not receive a letter in return, his self-confidence took a hit. He believed that he was going to be a bachelor for the rest of his life. He stated that he was never going to be satisfied with anyone that was blockhead enough to marry him.

It was during his second term as legislature that Lincoln became the floor leader of the Whig Party. He continued to live a simple life in a small room, eating little and living as cheaply as he could. He put every penny that he could toward the debts that he had inherited from his partner.

He moved to Springfield, Illinois, when the capital did and continued to study the law books. He took the bar exam and became a lawyer. At this point in his life, he still disliked his father and after leaving home never spoke to Thomas again.

Lincoln practiced law with his partner John Stewart. Then, when John Stewart ran for office, Lincoln was left to run the practice on his own. Abe was known as a brilliant man who was great at handling local arguments. There were, however, two problems. The first problem was that Abe was unable to defend a person if he knew they were guilty. The second problem was that he would often accept cases if he believed a person had been wronged, even though they could not pay him.

While he was debating in the legislature, he found that Stephen Douglas was usually his opponent. The two were alike in many ways. They were both great debaters, ambitious, and young. However, they were also completely opposite in other ways.

Lincoln supported a strong government while Douglas thought that the government should stay out of the state's business. They were completely opposite when it came to the way that they looked as well. Lincoln was tall with dark hair, while Douglas had blonde hair and was very short. The two men even came from different backgrounds. Lincoln, as we know, was poor growing up and not well-educated. Douglas, however, had grown up rich and received a great education.

When the two met each other for the first time, there was no way for them to know how much their rivalry would change the nation.

Lincoln and Douglas had both been introduced to Mary Todd, who was from Kentucky. Her father was a wealthy banker, and she was one of the most desired belles in the area. Lincoln, having given up on love, was quite surprised that he had feelings for Mary.

Most thought that Douglas would have been Mary's choice because he came from a wealthy family and he was refined. However, it was Abraham she fell in love with, and even though her family protested, in 1841 the two were engaged.

It seemed that Abraham loved Mary, however, he was very insecure. He knew that she would be miserable living in poverty. Her friends had told her that if she married him she was going to ruin her life. He feared that her friends were right, and soon depression set in again, causing him to end the engagement.

Just a few months later, one of Abe's friends married and told

Abe that he was the happiest man alive. This caused Abe to reconsider, and soon he and Mary met at a party. They spoke about his fears, and in 1842 the two were married.

Lincoln had been right to fear that living in poverty would affect Mary. Growing up, she had servants, but now she had to take care of the chores. Lincoln often had to leave her alone as he traveled for work, and by the time they had been married for a year they had a young son named Robert Todd Lincoln. Still, even through all the hardships, their love remained.

Soon, Abe was able to move his small family out of the one room that they were living in and purchase a house. The two added two more sons to their family, Edward and William Lincoln, however, neither boy would survive into their teenage years.

Lincoln was elected to Congress in 1847, and the family moved to Washington City. On December 6th of 1847, Lincoln took his seat in the House of Representatives. Upon arriving to the nation's capital, he realized that they still allowed slavery, and in 1849 he proposed that slavery be abolished.

Lincoln also believed that Polk, who was president at the time, was wrong in accusing Mexico for the bloodshed over the land in Texas. He was a patriot; however, he believed that

Polk was wrong, and he knew that speaking out about it could make him very unpopular.

When he spoke out about how the conflict began, many people saw Lincoln as unpatriotic, and his reelection efforts were not supported by the Whig Party. The family returned to Springfield, Lincoln believing that his career in politics was over.

Edward Lincoln died in 1850, just two months before he turned four. He had suffered from tuberculosis for 52 days. His death caused both Mary and Abe to suffer from a deep depression, but by the end of 1850, William had been born, and Thomas was born on April 4, 1853.

After four years of practicing law in Springfield, Lincoln decided that it was time for him to get back into politics. At that point, he realized that he did not agree with the Whig Party beliefs or policies, therefore, he formed his own party known as the Republican Party.

It was during the 1850s that people began focusing on the issue of slavery. The Northern states were filled with factories, which meant that they had no use for slaves and opposed it. However, the Southern states were filled with plantations and supported slavery. The Southerners feared that if they did not have slaves, they would not be able to work the fields, and they would be unable to survive.

Lincoln saw that the issue was causing division in the states. He knew that if the nation was going to survive, everyone had to work together. There was no way the nation could survive if it was divided against itself.

In fact, when he was accepting the Republican Party nomination for the Senate in 1858, he stated, "A house divided against itself cannot stand." He believed that the nation could not withstand half of the states being free and half being slave. He said that he did not expect the nation to fall, but he did expect that it would cease if it was divided. It had to be either slave or free.

Lincoln's opponent was Stephen Douglas, who believed that it was up to the states to decide if they wanted to allow slavery or not. Douglas ended up winning the election. Even though Lincoln had lost the election, he had the attention of the nation and soon become the Republican candidate for the presidency. Douglas was his opponent, but there was another Democratic candidate. Because there were two Democratic candidates, the votes were split between the two, which resulted in Lincoln being voted in as the 16th US president.

Upon his election, the South felt that their way of life was threatened, and they did not believe that a man who wanted to abolish slavery could represent them. South Carolina was the first to leave the Union. Ten other states followed and created the Confederate States of America. This allowed them to make their own laws and allowed them to control their own lives.

The US government sent a shipment of supplies to Fort Sumter, and shots were fired by the Confederate troops. Those were the first shots of the Civil War.

The Union knew that their soldiers were better trained and that they had the seaports and industry to help support them. They believed that they were going to be able to win easily. However, the war was not easy at all.

Lincoln was horrified that the nation was falling apart during his presidency. He tried to compromise with the South, asking that they phase out slavery so that it would not affect the economy, but the Confederacy wanted nothing to do with this proposal.

He was also facing personal problems. Mary was more than happy to have moved into the White House, yet in remodeling it, she ran up about 27,000 dollars in debt which would be almost 800,000 dollars today. The spending caused tension between the two, but on top of this, William died in 1862, which only added to the stress the president was under.

Thousands of men from both the North and the South were killed during the war. Lincoln slipped back into depression, and he knew that the troops were struggling as well. He decided that he would sign the Emancipation Proclamation on the 22nd of September 1862, which would free all of the slaves on January 1, 1863.

However, the war had not ended by the 1st of January 1863, and the Emancipation Proclamation had no effect. Lincoln was unable to eat, he couldn't sleep, and he spent hours waiting for information about the war.

People began to hate the president as well as the war. He received death threats, yet he believed in what his mother had told him so long ago: he was destined to do great things. If he had been destined to die, he would have when he was a boy.

In 1863, Lincoln was informed that a huge battle was going to take place at Gettysburg. He was sure that this battle would determine the winner of the war. Lincoln stayed in the telegraph office for three days waiting on word when finally, he was informed that the Union had won.

He went to the battlefield at Gettysburg and gave the Gettysburg Address. He had been right. The battle was a turning point in the war. People begin to have hope that the war would end soon, and Lincoln was elected to a second term in 1864.

In April 1865, General Robert E. Lee surrendered, and the nation began to heal. Lincoln called for peace and forgiveness within the nation; however, the Southerners hated him. He had destroyed everything that they had worked for, and the

Northerners thought that those in the South should have been punished for causing the war.

Just five days after General Robert E. Lee surrendered, John Wilkes Booth fired one shot from a single-shot Derringer, shooting the President in the head just below his left ear and killing him.

President Andrew Johnson

Andrew Johnson was not elected as president. Instead, he took the office after the assassination of Abraham Lincoln since he was the vice president at the time. He was sworn into office just hours after Lincoln had died.

Johnson had grown up poor in North Carolina and had not been able to attend school as a young boy. His family was far too poor, and there was simply no time for him to worry about an education.

At the age of 14, he was sent to work for a tailor. He learned how to make clothes by working very hard and eventually opened his own business in Tennessee. At the age of 18, he married Eliza, who taught him how to read and write.

Soon, he became involved in politics, and at 21 he was elected to the town council. In just two years, he was elected mayor. When he was 35 years old, he was elected to Congress. Afterwards, he was elected governor of Tennessee and then senator.

Andrew Johnson was part of the Democratic Party and supported the Democratic Party's candidate in the 1860 election. He did not support Lincoln. However, as we know, Lincoln was elected president.

Of course, after the election, the Southern states began leaving the Union, forming a nation of their own. Johnson did not support the succession, but instead believed that the South needed to remain part of the Union. At this point, he had no other choice—he had to support Lincoln.

The citizens of Tennessee disagreed with Johnson and decided that they would join the Confederacy. Johnson, in order to save his own life, had to flee his home, only returning once the Union had taken control of the state. The Union made Johnson the military governor.

This was when Lincoln took notice of Johnson. He saw a man that stood up for the Union even in the face of opposition. When Lincoln decided to run for a second term, it was Johnson whom he chose to be his vice president. It was Lincoln's hope that Johnson would be able to win the support of those Democrats who loved the Union. He also hoped that Johnson would be able to help bring healing to the relationship between the North and the South.

Once Lincoln was assassinated, Johnson took the role as president, and it was up to him to determine how to rebuild the Union. It was Johnson who would determine if the Union would show mercy to the Southern states and whether the rebuilding of the nation would be easy or difficult.

The Republican Party wanted the South to be punished for taking part in the rebellion. He wanted legislation passed against the South. They believed that Johnson would agree with them because he had called the South rebels and traitors. He had stated that it was time for Americans to understand what crime was and to understand that it would not go unpunished.

Johnson, however, surprised many of the Republicans by announcing that all of the confederates who promised to obey the laws and support the union would be pardoned for their crimes. He even allowed those who had been officials in the Confederacy to hold office.

This caused the Republicans to become very angry. They believed that Johnson was too soft, and that allowing the Confederate officials to run for office proved that nothing had changed. They wanted the rebels punished.

One newspaper article stated that there was only one way to ensure the future of the nation and that was to allow the North to dictate what happened in the entire nation. Southerners were not to be trusted, and they should be punished for their treason.

The Republicans were also worried about what was going to happen to all the slaves who had been freed. They did not believe that the governments in the southern states would treat blacks equally. They used recent legislature that had passed in the South as proof.

One of the laws dictated that in the state of Mississippi, a black person was not allowed to rent farmland, and a black person had to have permission to work a job other than farming. The law also stated that if a black person did not have another job, they would be forced to work for a white person, which was usually the black person's former owner. Blacks were also not allowed to vote.

The Republicans believed that the reconstruction program created by Johnson had to be stopped. They quickly set out to take control of Congress in order to get their own program passed. They knew that the only way they would be able to punish the South was to gain political power.

They began by refusing to let a lot of the southern congressmen who had been recently elected take their seats in Congress. They also formed a committee that would make the decisions about the reconstruction program instead of the Senate or the House.

Congress also created an agency that would ensure black refugees from the South were provided with food and clothing since they were former slaves who did not have jobs, money, or food. They also started teaching the black refugees how to read and write.

Republicans wanted to increase the powers of the agency and passed a bill which was sent to the president for approval, but it was vetoed. Johnson stated that the bill would have created a false hope among the freed slaves, and he stated that it was also unconstitutional. The Republicans tried to overturn the veto; however, they were unable to get the votes needed.

Congress did pass several bills that allowed the government to protect the rights of the freed slaves who were in the southern states, but Johnson vetoed those bills as well, claiming that they interfered with the rights of each state.

This made the Republicans even angrier. The newspapers had begun attacking the president and his policies, some articles even accusing Johnson of treason. These stories, of course, influenced the way that the American people felt about the president.

The American people agreed with the Republicans, and in the congressional elections of 1866, they gave the majority of the power to the Republicans. This allowed them to pass any bill they desired, because even if Johnson vetoed it, they had the numbers to overturn the veto.

Pushing as far as they could, the Republicans tried to remove

Johnson from office. Under the Constitution, the House has the right to bring charges against any president, and the Senate acting as a jury determines if the president is guilty of the charges. If two-thirds of the senators believe that the president is guilty, they can then have him removed from office.

Eleven charges were brought against Johnson, most of them being based on the fact that he had removed his Secretary of War from office. According to the law, Johnson was not allowed to remove any officer from the cabinet without getting the approval of the Senate first. He was also charged with criticizing Congress, dishonoring Congress, and dishonoring the presidency.

The trial began on March 5, 1868. Johnson refused to attend, but his lawyers did. Each senator swore to be just, promising that they would give the president a fair and honest trial. Many accusations were made, but there was little evidence provided to support any of the charges.

Johnson's lawyers pointed this out, calling for emotions to be set to the side and facts presented. According to the Constitution, they had to prove that Johnson had committed a crime. It was stated that Johnson had not committed a crime but that the trial was completely political.

The Senate was warned of the repercussions. No future president would ever be safe from removal if the House or

Senate opposed his views.

The trial went on and on. Out of the 54 votes, 36 were needed to remove Johnson from office. It was obvious that 35 of the votes were going to be against Johnson. Seven of the Senators were undecided. If just one of them voted against Johnson, he would be impeached. Just days before the vote was to take place, six out of the seven senators stated that they were going to vote not guilty. One senator remained. One vote would determine the future of the president and the nation

On May 16th, the votes were taken, and 35 voted that Johnson was guilty and 19 not guilty. It had come down to one vote, and Johnson would remain president.

The small group of senators who did not vote against Johnson were denounced by the other senators as well as by the newspapers. They were referred to as traitors, condemned by friends and family as well as their supporters, and none of them were re-elected.

They had done what they thought was right, even though they had to deal with millions cursing at them. However, they knew that one day, Americans would know that they had saved the nation from a great threat.

The removal of Johnson from office would have meant that if the president did not have the approval of Congress, he could have been removed. In other words, instead of having a president, we would have a prime minister. Johnson's victory ensured that it was not Congress who determined who the president was, but instead it was the people.

The Republicans were able to get a lot of support by helping to give freed slaves the right to vote. They knew that the freed slaves would vote with the party that had freed them. They also passed a law stating that if a southerner had taken part in the rebellion, they could not vote. This meant that the majority of southerners were unable to vote against the Republicans.

Strong laws were also made when it came to what the southerners had to do in order to re-enter the Union. Each state had to have a new constitution which protected the voting rights of all freed black men. They also had to approve an amendment which would give the blacks citizenship.

They helped to organize a group of blacks for the Republican Party. Many of the men of the South hated the Republicans and called them carpetbaggers. The name came from the fact that when the northern Republicans would travel to the South, they would carry all of their possessions in a carpet handbag. It was not meant to be a friendly nickname, and it is a name that we still hear today.

Those in the South had the right to be angry. They had lost the war, and they had lost their power and their way of life, but there was more to the story. Many of the new officials who represented the southern states were not from the South, but instead, they were Republicans who had ceased control. Some of these new officials were very dishonest and only used their new positions to pad their pocketbooks.

For example, the new governor of South Carolina was from Ohio. He had been a former officer in the Union army, and he provided dishonest men with government jobs. Some of the men were even criminals. The governor of Louisiana was from Illinois, and after serving for four years he had over one million dollars, even though he had only officially earned $32,000 the entire time.

Of course, it was not only in the South that government officials were corrupt. However, this was the beginning of the corruption.

President Ulysses S. Grant

We all know that Ulysses Grant was the 18th president of the United States who served two terms, and he was a commander in the Union army during the Civil War; however, many people forget that he was an amazing author as well.

Mark Twain stated that there was no higher piece of literature than Grant's personal memoirs. The story of why he wrote his memoirs is just as amazing as the story of his life.

Grant became an author at the end of his life. This was after he had become a partner in Grant and Ward, which was a bank that Ferdinand Ward had founded. The problem was that Ward only used Grant's name in order to attract investors. The truth was that Ward was operating a Ponzi scheme. Grant had thought that he was going to get rich off the bank, but Ward ended up fleeing with all of the money, even Grant's.

Not long afterward, Grant was hit with another blow. He loved smoking cigars but found that they had caused him to develop throat cancer. The doctors did not expect him to live very long. Julia, his wife, was his main concern when he found out that he had cancer. He cared only that his family was facing poverty.

He was broke thanks to Ward and was battling cancer, so in order to ensure that his family was taken care of, he decided that he would write his life story. He negotiated a contract with Mark Twain in which he would receive 10,000 dollars in advance as well as 20 percent of the sales. Grant was saved financially and delivered his memoirs to Twain days before his death, ensuring that his family had financial security.

Despite being in excruciating pain, he wrote three pages per day for the entire last year that he lived. Many refer to this as his bravest fight. Grant spent about six to seven hours each day writing, but in the last few weeks of his life, he had to dictate to his assistant by whispering in his ear. He knew that his time was running out as he wrote the preface, saying that he wished he had more time so that he could satisfy the expectations of the public.

He used every ounce of energy that he had to write the book, knowing that he was dying. He told a friend of his that he prayed God would allow him to finish his book before he died.

Ulysses S. Grant was born Hiram Ulysses Grant, however, when he went to West Point there was a mistake made and his name was changed to Ulysses Simpson Grant. His mother Hannah's maiden name was Simpson, and she had used her connections in order to get him into West Point. Ulysses did not have the error corrected and became Ulysses S. Grant. To his friends, he was Sam.

Grant graduated 21st out of a class of 39 in 1843, served as quartermaster throughout the Mexican War, and was known for being able to get supplies across the toughest terrain. He was also known for disobeying orders and going to the front lines when in battle. After the Mexican War, Grant was posted on the West Coast and given the rank of Captain. He was forced to resign on the 31st of July in 1854 because he was suspected of drinking heavily.

Many still debate just how much Grant drank, especially while he fought in the Civil War. It is known that he did drink because he regularly had severe migraines. Many people believe this is why there are so many reports of him being drunk.

On top of this, he was probably bored with frontier duty, and he most likely missed Julia a great deal which could have led to increased alcohol consumption. John A. Rollins was Grant's ade-de-camp, who had watched his own father drink his family into poverty growing up and saw the drinking lead to the death of his father.

He told Grant that the first time the commander saw him drunk would be the last time he would serve as his aide. Rollins, however, was still Grant's aide at the end of the Civil War.

Julia was from St. Louis, Missouri, and married Grant on the 22nd of August 1848. The two had been introduced to each other by James Longstreet, who was a friend of Grant's. Longstreet was a General in the Confederate Army while Grant was rising in the ranks of the Union. Even though they had fought on different sides, they were friends, and Grant even convinced Hayes to appoint Longstreet as the ambassador of the Ottoman Empire in 1880.

After Grant resigned from the Army, he tried several different ventures. He opened a farm in Missouri, having one slave his father-in-law had given to him, but the farm failed, and Grant emancipated the slave. He could have sold the man, whose name was William Jones. Even though he was in debt, he chose not to do so.

When the Civil War began, Grant was living in Galena, Illinois, with his wife and children. He was not commissioned into the Army initially; however, Congressman Washburne helped to get him named Colonel on the 17th of June 1861.

This took him back to Missouri, and while he was there, he used the money that he earned to pay off old debts. The first battle he led his troops into was in Belmont, Missouri, on the 7th of November 1861. Initially, he saw success, but when the Confederate reinforcements arrived, he had to withdraw his men.

Later, he and his troops took Fort Henry and Fort Donelson, where Simon Bunker—who was a Confederate general and Grant's old friend—asked what the terms for surrender were. Grant told him that nothing but unconditional and immediate surrender would be accepted. This statement resulted in him being called Unconditional Surrender Grant. The nickname was also inspired by his initials. He was then promoted to Major General.

Grant was removed from command temporarily because a Confederate sympathizer who worked at the telegraph office intercepted messages he was sending to the War Department and destroyed them. This resulted in him not being able to communicate with his superiors. However, after it was discovered what had happened, he was reinstated.

There was one point when Lincoln had to reprimand Grant in December 1862. Grant's father had brought several friends when he came to visit his son. These men were cotton speculators. A cotton speculator was a man who would travel ahead of the Union armies and buy all of the cotton at a very low price then sell it for a huge profit to factories in the North that had no cotton.

It happened that some of the men his father brought with him were Jewish. Grant was never known to be an anti-Semitic man; however, he issued the Jewish Order, Order Number 11. It stated that the Jews were violating the regulation of trade and that they were to all be expelled from the military district that Grant oversaw within 24 hours.

Grant was usually a very quiet man; however, it was known that he could have a temper. This order was seen as an outburst. Later, he admitted that the criticism he faced was deserved. When he was elected as president, he appointed several Jews to positions of power, which resulted in him carrying the Jewish vote later in 1868.

It was in 1869 that Grant, the Republican candidate, won the election. He had been courted by both parties but had run as the Republican candidate.

Grant was very honest, and although there were many scandals in his administration, he was not involved in them. In 1872, he was re-elected. During Grant's second term, the US faced one of the worst financial crises ever. It was called the Panic of 1873, and it was due to the Jay Cooke Company Bank and over-speculation of railroads. The bank had sold bonds during the war to the Union; however, they were unable to pay the money back.

The Republican Party tried to get Grant to serve as candidate for a third term in 1880; however, they failed.

It was Ulysses S. Grant Jr., known as Buck, who borrowed 100,000 dollars from Grant in order to enter the partnership with Ward. Just three years after, Ward asked to borrow 150,000 dollars for only 24 hours. Grant, did not have the money to give to his son and borrowed it. Ward, however, did not return the money but instead absconded with it.

Grant had to sell his properties and possessions in order to pay the money back. It was then that he began writing about the experiences he had during the Civil War for Century magazine. Soon, he was in contact with Mark Twain and began writing his memoirs after being diagnosed with throat cancer.

President Rutherford B. Hayes

Hayes took office in 1877. He was the president during the period after the Civil War known as Reconstruction. Hayes was known as a dignified and honest man, even though at the time his political ideas were radical. Hayes was moderate when it came to policies except for the fact that he banned all liquor from the White House during his presidency.

Hayes' father died before he was born, and it was not long after that his brother died as well. This meant that as he was growing up, it was just him, his mother, and his sister. Later, one of his uncles helped to raise him.

Hayes was called Rudd when he was growing up in Ohio on a farm. He spent his childhood playing with his sister. She taught him to read, and he fell in love with books. Hayes attended school at Kenyon College as well as Harvard Law.

He started out as a lawyer in Cincinnati, Ohio, but because he defended the poor and those who were in difficult situations, he did not make much money. It was during this time that he courted Lucy Webb. He eventually married Lucy, and she, like his sister and his mother, was able to influence his thinking.

When he married, his views were moderate. This means that he was more of a middle-of-the-road man than he was a Republican or a Democrat. Lucy, however, was very much against slavery and alcohol. She took part in the movements to ban alcohol in the US. She also encouraged her husband to defend the poor as well as runaway slaves.

The two created a marriage where each partner was equal and they focused on helping other people. They were also known as friendly people who were welcoming and informal. The two had eight children, but only five survived. Lucy described her husband as a calm father who took the time to care for his children no matter how busy he was.

During the election, Hayes represented the Republicans, and the Democrats were represented by Samuel Tilden. This election would turn out to be a very hostile one because Tilden won the popular vote; however, Hayes won the electoral votes. There was also a problem with some of the Southern states. It was unclear which of them had won Louisiana, South Carolina, and Florida. It took until March of the following year before the winner was decided, which was only days before the president was supposed to be sworn into office.

Some stated that the Democrats in the Southern states had not allowed many of the black men to vote, and had they been allowed to vote they would have voted for Hayes.

Hayes was also considered an independent who was not loyal to either party. One of the first things that Hayes did after he took office was probably one of the most important things he ever did, and that was to withdraw the troops from the South.

While the troops' job was to protect the rights of the blacks, the white Democrats were not happy that the government was involved in the affairs of the states. The troops were also not very good at doing their jobs.

Hayes stated that if the Southern states agreed to keep the laws and to treat every person equally, he would withdraw the troops. The Southern officials agreed, and the Reconstruction came to an end. However, as time went on, the rights of blacks were violated at an alarming rate.

It was because of this that Hayes' legacy would be one of betrayal. It was his system that would allow for racism and violence to continue.

Before Hayes took office, Congress members would generally provide government jobs for their political allies. Of course, these jobs came with a great wage. Hayes wanted the rules to change. He believed that the jobs should be given to those who were most qualified to do them.

This angered the members of Congress. The Democrats wanted to ensure that Hayes was unable to do this and tried to stop him from vetoing the bills that were passed through Congress; however, Hayes fought them, and he won.

By the time his third year in office began, Hayes had helped to restore some of the trust in the US government that the

Americans had lost under Johnson and Grant. He also worked to ease tensions between the Northern states and Southern states. Hayes worked hard to stabilize the economy, and he helped to pave the way for civil service reform.

Today, we do not remember Hayes as one of the greatest presidents; however, he was not one of the worst either. Hayes was somewhere in the middle, just like his political beliefs. Many believe that if he had a second term, he would have been remembered as a great president. Hayes, however, had promised the American people that he would only serve one term, and being true to his word, he did not run for a second term.

Hayes had always believed that the best way to improve the nation was to focus on the education system. When he retired, he took on the role of president of two different social welfare programs. One of the programs focused on providing a Christian education to the blacks in Southern states.

He also focused on reforming the prison system after he retired. Hayes became ill when he was 70 and died from heart failure. It was one of his sons who created the new tradition of a presidential library in honor of Hayes.

James A. Garfield

James A. Garfield had been president for just four months when he headed out for a holiday. While he had only been president for a short time, things had not been easy for him. It started with a clash with the Republicans, and then his wife became ill, suffering from malaria, and almost died. Once she was feeling better, Garfield was ready to go to New England on holiday.

James G. Blaine, who was the Secretary of State at the time, rode with Garfield to the train station. At that time, presidents did not have bodyguards.

As Garfield's carriage pulled up to the train station, Charles Guiteau was in the waiting room pacing back and forth. He believed that God had sent him on a mission. Guiteau was 39 at the time and had been stalking Garfield for weeks waiting for the perfect chance to kill him.

Most people that knew Guiteau believed he was mentally insane, but that did not stop him from planning the crime in detail. Guiteau had purchased a .44 caliber ivory-handled pistol specifically to assassinate the president because he believed that it would one day be placed in a museum. He had assumed that he would be sent to the district jail after the assassination (only for a short period until he was released, since he was doing the work of God) and tried to take a tour of it at one point. Many believe that he was interested in what his new home would be like.

He also carried a letter in his pocket during the assassination which stated that he was doing God's will and it was the only way to save the Republic.

At about 9:20 AM on July 2, 1881, Garfield walked into the train station with Blaine, who was escorting him to his train. As the men walked through the station, Guiteau walked up behind them and pulled out his pistol. He fired two shots. The first just grazed the president's arm, causing him to shout out. The second shot fired hit Garfield in the back and knocked him to the floor.

As the shots rang out, panic filled the station. Guiteau tried to flee, taking advantage of the panic that he had caused. However, a man was blocking the door which allowed a police officer and a ticket agent to stop Guiteau. As soon as the passengers realized what had happened, they began to shout for him to be lynched. Guiteau requested that the police take him to the jailhouse for his own safety, which they did.

While all of this was going on, Garfield was lying on the floor of the train station bleeding from the wound. It only took a matter of minutes for ten doctors to arrive and begin examining him in order to locate the bullet.

At that time, no one realized that the bullet had not hit any of his vital organs or arteries and that the injury was survivable. The doctors only made the situation worse by using unsterilized instruments as well as their germ covered fingers to try and find the bullet.

In doing so, they introduced all sorts of germs into the wound and probably caused the infection that would eventually kill him. After the president had dealt with the doctors digging into the wound for about an hour, he was taken back to the White House. The doctors did not think he was going to live through the night, but he pretended to be brave for the sake of his children, telling them that he was going to be fine and fighting with all of his strength.

Over the following days, Garfield fought for his life as the public learned about Charles J. Guiteau. He had grown up in Illinois and had spent most of his life as a drifter. He had tried many different careers and had failed at all of them.

Guiteau considered himself to be an extreme Republican and had even written a speech on the behalf of Garfield during the election. The speech was ignored, but somehow Guiteau believed that it was his speech that got Garfield elected.

After the inauguration, he moved to D.C. and began visiting the White House regularly. He had even managed to meet with Garfield at one point. It was during this meeting that Guiteau told the president about the speech and asked that he be reward by being named to the consulship in Paris. Garfield denied the request, which angered Guiteau, and soon he began focusing on getting revenge on the president.

One night as Guiteau was lying in bed, he had what he called a flash of inspiration from God. He believed that God himself wanted him to kill Garfield. It was from this point forward that he believed the only way to save the country was to kill Garfield and ensure that Chester A. Arthur, the vice president, took his place.

Even after Guiteau was arrested, he believed that Arthur would rescue him. He told detectives that if they stuck with him, they would be made the Chiefs of Police because Arthur and all of the men were his friends.

Throughout the summer, the newspapers printed updates on the president's condition. Garfield had fought hard the first few days after he had been shot, but after his doctor gave him a dose of morphine, quinine, and alcohol, he began vomiting and was left emaciated and weak.

The doctor also continued to try and find the bullet, even having Alexander Graham Bell use a metal detector on Garfield to find the bullet. The problem was, however, that the metal detector kept picking up on the springs in the mattress, and Bell was only allowed to check the right side of the President's body because that was where the doctor believed the bullet was located. The doctor, however, was wrong.

By the time September arrived, Garfield was suffering from a severe infection that had probably been caused by the unsanitary conditions of the medical equipment used on him. He suffered from abscesses all over his body, as well as a fever that could not be reduced. The president was taken to the Jersey shore to stay in a cottage in hopes that the sea air would provide him with some relief, but on September 19, 1881, Garfield died, only 200 days after his inauguration.

The nation mourned their leader, and 10.000 people showed up to view his body. Soon, however, the people became focused on punishing the assassin. There were two attempts on his life, and the court had to interview over 150 candidates before they were able to find twelve impartial men to form the jury.

Guiteau plead not guilty by reason of insanity, claiming that the assassination had been an act of God, not of his own. He even tried to push the blame onto the doctors, stating that while he had shot the president, it was the doctors who had killed him.

This was a very good point. It is believed that if it had not been for the medicine that was used at the time, as well as the lack of sterile instruments used on the president, he would have lived, but this theory was not going to save Guiteau.

In less than one hour, the jury returned with a guilty verdict, and on June 30, 1881, just a few days before the one-year mark from when the president had been shot, Guiteau was hanged in Washington D.C.

RANDOM FUN FACTS

1. James Polk, knowing that many other politicians wanted to run for the presidency, made a promise that if the people elected him as president, he would only serve one term. He kept that promise and did not run for a second term.
2. Andrew Johnson was the first president to have been impeached, even though he was not removed from the office.
3. Some of the scandals that occurred during Ulysses S. Grant's time in office included the Whiskey Ring, the Credit Mobilizer, and Black Friday.
4. Some believed that the only reason Hayes became the president—even though he had not received the popular vote—was because he had agreed to the Compromise of 1877, which officially ended the Reconstruction.
5. Franklin Pierce signed the Kansas-Nebraska Act and also allowed open trade with Japan for the first time since the nation was formed.
6. Rutherford Hays stated that no one had ever left the presidency with less regret than he did.
7. James Garfield was the last President of the United States

to be born in a log cabin.

8. Millard Fillmore married his teacher from the New Hope Academy when he was just 19 years old. Abigail, however, was only two years older than him.
9. Franklin Peirce did not swear his oath to the office nor did he place his hand on a Bible. Instead, he affirmed his oath and placed his hand on a law book.
10. Abraham Lincoln was challenged by a local bully, Jack Armstrong, to a wrestling match after he moved to New Salem in 1831. Many people gathered to watch and place bets on Armstrong and Lincoln. Honest Abe won.
11. Andrew Johnson had drunk a large amount of whiskey before his inauguration, and it is said that during his speech, it was quite obvious that he was drunk.
12. Ulysses S. Grant received a twenty dollar speeding ticket for riding a horse too fast.
13. Hayes not only banned alcohol from the White House in order to please his wife, but it is said that he was trying to get support from the Prohibitionists as well.
14. James Garfield was the first president to be able to write with both his right and left hand. It is also believed that he was able to write Latin with one hand and Greek with the other.

15. James Polk waged the Mexican War, and as a result of the victory, Arizona, California, Colorado, New Mexico, Nevada, Wyoming, and Utah were added to the US.

TEST YOURSELF- QUESTIONS AND ANSWERS

1. Which President was nicknamed Old Rough and Ready?

   A. Polk

   B. Fillmore

   C. Taylor

2. Which President signed the Fugitive Slave Law?

   A) Pierce

   B) Taylor

   C) Fillmore

3. Who helped to form the Republican Party?

   A) Lincoln

   B) Grant

   C) Johnson

4. Which President didn't swear his oath of office?

   A) Garfield

   B) Pierce

   C) Buchanan

5. Who banned alcohol from the White House?

   A) Garfield

   B) Grant

   C) Hayes

ANSWERS

1. B
2. C
3. A
4. B
5. C

CHAPTER THREE

LIBERTY, JUSTICE, AND PROGRESSIVISM

When we talk about the Progressive Era, we are talking about a period in time when a variety of reforms took place through the US. Not only were the changes generated on a national level, but there were a lot of local changes as well. Some of the areas included prohibition, the regulation of child labor, women's suffrage, the expansion of the education system, social services, and much more.

It was not only the political leaders who were progressives, but it was also educators, farmers, businessmen, and academics. They believed that it was the responsibility of the government at all levels to solve economic, social, and political problems.

President Chester A. Arthur

Chester Alan Arthur took office after the death of James Garfield in March 1881. The two men had not been close, and while they did belong to the same political party, they had different ideas when it came to the issues that were being faced. They had even had public disagreements on several different topics.

If Garfield had not been assassinated, Arthur would probably have not have had much of a voice, but Garfield did die, and Arthur became the President of the United States. He served as president for the remaining of what would have been Garfield's term, which was about three and a half years. According to historians, Arthur was a competent president.

Arthur grew up in Vermont and then New York. He had seven siblings. His father was strongly opposed to slavery and worked as a religious leader. Arthur went to college in New York, and then he taught while he studied law. He, however, had no intention of staying in the small town nor living modestly. Arthur wanted to live in New York City. He wanted to be a wealthy lawyer, and he wanted to be a public official. He was determined to enjoy the gentleman's lifestyle. That was exactly what he did too.

During the Civil War, Arthur went from having an entry level job at a local law office to being a leader in the military. After the war ended, he landed a job as a lawyer that paid well until he was offered a top position working in the government, which he accepted.

The job was tax collector, which he did for seven years, acting as supervisor over a thousand people. Under Arthur's supervision, the group collected a large amount of money in taxes from imported products.

Arthur was under the supervision of Roscoe Conkling, who was the New York senator. Conkling was known for trading political support for financial favors as well as other favors. While Arthur was never proven guilty of accepting any money, he was very closely linked to Conkling.

When Hayes focused on fighting the corruption that was taking place in the government jobs in 1878, it was Arthur and Conkling that he targeted.

Hayes had actually removed Arthur from his job, and in order to get it back, Arthur and Conkling put their efforts toward getting Grant re-elected. When this failed and James Garfield was given the nomination, something had to be done.

Arthur and Garfield were not allies even though they were both part of the Republican Party. The two had completely different opinions on the issues. Because the political leaders at the time were trying to unite the party, they chose Arthur as the nominee for vice president.

This plan worked great when it came to ensuring that the election was won. Republicans, even though they were a split party, felt that the team stood for what they believed in. However, the two men did not have a good relationship.

One of the first things that Garfield did when he took office was to appoint someone else to Arthur's previous job in New York. He made sure that he appointed someone who was not affiliated with nor loyal to Conkling. Instead, he gave the position to one of his own supporters.

In an attempt to protest this action, Conkling resigned. The situation suddenly changed when Garfield was shot and Chester A. Arthur became the President of the United States.

When he took office, the public believed that he was an experienced politician. Most of them, however, believed that he was going to focus on supporting the goals of a very small group within the Republican Party.

To their surprise, he took a moderate position on many issues. This was in total opposition to his party. He did support the reform of the nation's civil service as well as cleaning up the corruption that was within the government. He even took away the ability for politicians to give their supporters government jobs.

His actions did actually help the Republican Party in the short term. However, he broke away from the Republican Party when it came to many issues. He eventually vetoed the anti-immigration act that had passed through Congress which would have not allowed any Chinese to immigrate to the US for 20 years.

Arthur knew that the Chinese had helped to improve the economy in the US by helping to build the railroad system, and he did not want to hurt any future trades with China. However, when Congress then offered to reduce the ban to 10 years, he agreed. On top of that, he banned all immigrants that were criminals, mentally insane, or considered poor.

One of the acts he is most known for was hiring Louis Tiffany to redecorate the White House, making it brighter and more stylish. After it was redecorated, Arthur held parties for the elite. He was given the nickname The Gentleman Boss.

He was not a terrible president. In fact, he did quite well while in office. He did not try to run for a second term, but instead returned to New York after his term was over. He tried to continue working as a lawyer, but soon after leaving office he became too ill to work. Arthur died at the age of 57 years at his home in New York.

President Grover Cleveland

We seem to have grown accustomed to sex scandals in the White House, but when Cleveland was president, this was not something that people expected to happen. Most of us know Cleveland as the only president to ever serve two terms in office non-consecutively. He is remembered as an honest president and a courageous man. Some also remember him for marrying the young daughter of his best friend; however, that is another story.

What many people do not know is that Cleveland, along with his aides, covered up allegations of what we would consider today to be date rape.

It was the 15th of December in 1873 when a woman named Maria Halpin was walking down Swan Street in Buffalo, New York. She came across Cleveland, who was out for a stroll. The two of them knew each other well; he had been courting her for several months. The two greeted each other, and then Cleveland invited Maria to join him for dinner. Maria later recalled that Cleveland was persistent that she join him.

The two enjoyed a pleasant meal at the Ocean Dining Hall and Oyster House, and then Cleveland walked Maria back to the boarding house where she was staying. At this point, Cleveland sexually assaulted the woman using force and, according to Maria, without her consent.

She then stated that he threatened to ruin her, even if it cost him $10,000 and if it resulted in his hanging. Maria claimed that she told Cleveland that she never wanted to see him again and insisted he leave her room. He left, but just six weeks later, Maria found out that she was pregnant.

Maria gave birth to a baby boy on the 14th of September in 1874 in a hospital in Buffalo for unwed mothers. She named the boy Oscar Folsom Cleveland after Folsom, who was

Cleveland's best friend. (Later, Cleveland would marry Folsom's daughter even though he was 27 years older than she.)

What happened next seems to have come out of a horror story. Cleveland had the boy taken from his mother and put into the Buffalo Orphan Asylum. He had Maria placed into the Providence Lunatic Asylum. She was, however, released after her initial evaluation, as the doctors concluded that she was not mentally insane. They realized that she had been incarcerated due to the abuse of power by one of the political elites.

Cleveland was then voted in as the Mayor of Buffalo, the following year he became the Governor of New York, and just two years later he was the Democrat nominee for the presidency.

Once Cleveland's name was on the ticket, journalists quickly dug up information about his illegitimate son and began smearing his campaign. The people who worked for Cleveland put the word out that Maria Halpin was nothing more than a sexual plaything. They said that she drank excessively and had been intimate with at least three, maybe even four other men, all of whom were married.

They claimed that Cleveland had taken responsibility for the boy because he was the only man that Maria Halpin had been intimate with who was not married. He saw his actions as the most courageous thing that he could do. His PR also stated that he did not have anything to do with the boy because he had doubts that he was the father.

According to research, Maria Halpin was a respected chaste woman who had been widowed and left with two young children. She attended church regularly, and everyone who knew her spoke highly of her. It is doubtful that Maria was willingly intimate with any man after the death of her husband.

In 1902, Maria died, having 200 dollars and a name that was forever going to be linked to shame. Her daughter stated that as Maria lay on her deathbed, she told her daughter to not allow her funeral to be public. She did not want strangers gazing upon her face, remembering her as the mistress of Cleveland. She requested that everything be done in quiet so that she could finally rest.

This was not the only scandal Cleveland was involved in. When Cleveland took office, he was a bachelor. This was only the third time this had ever happened. Cleveland married during his first term as president and was the first president to be married inside of the White House.

It was his marriage that was a bit of a scandal because the young woman he married was not only almost 30 years younger than he, but he was actually her legal guardian. It was not so strange at the time for a man to marry a woman that was much younger than he was; however, it was quite odd for a man to marry a girl he had been given guardianship over.

The girl was only 11 years old when her father had died. The man was Cleveland's best friend and had named Cleveland as her financial protector. This means that while he did not raise the girl, he had been her godfather.

Cleveland married Frances Folsom right after she turned 21, which surprised a lot of people because it would have been more acceptable had Cleveland married the widow of his friend. Cleveland called Frances "Frank", and the two began having children soon after they were married.

The first child they had was Ruth, but she only lived to the age of 12 due to being a very sickly child. About 20 years later, the Curtiss Candy Company change the name of the Kandy Kake candy bar to Baby Ruth in honor of Ruth Cleveland. However, because this happened when Babe Ruth was rising to fame, many believed that the company was trying to capitalize on his fame. They believed that the company claimed they had changed the name of the candy bar to honor Ruth Cleveland so that they would not have to pay royalties to Babe Ruth. In fact, a separate candy company had created a candy bar called the Babe Ruth with the approval of Babe Ruth. They were sued by the Curtiss Candy Company who won the lawsuit because the names were too similar. The other company had to stop production of the candy bar.

President Benjamin Harrison

Benjamin Harrison is not mentioned in the majority of history books, and when he is, he is not shown in a flattering light. It has even been written by historians that Benjamin Harrison would probably be remembered better if he, like his grandfather William Henry Harrison, had died during his first month in office.

Harrison was the 23rd President of the US and laid the foundations that Theodore Roosevelt would need to make some very important changes during his term.

One of these acts was that he signed the Sherman Antitrust Act, which later formed the foundation of Roosevelt's trust busting. He also focused on conservation, creating what would eventually become our National Forests, and he was the first president to fight for the protection of an animal.

During the election, Harrison did not win the popular vote. However, he received the electoral votes needed to be elected. He lost the popular vote not because he was not a popular candidate but because at the time, the Republican black votes had been suppressed in the South. He outpolled Cleveland in every other state though.

The Republican Party only controlled Congress for two years during Harrison's term. This meant that a lot of the legislation he tried to pass was blocked, yet he was still able to secure laws on many different issues such as veteran's pensions and postal subsidies. It was even said that never had Congress during peacetime passed so many measures that would be of long-lasting value to the Americans.

The Republicans lost the House of Representatives in 1890, not because the president had failed to deliver on his promises or because the party was not supported, but instead because the party had done so well. Since the Republican Party had done so well, the Republican voters did not feel the need to be as active.

President William McKinley

McKinley was the 25th president. Grover Cleveland served his second term between Harrison and McKinley and would be the only president to this day to serve two nonconsecutive terms.

When McKinley died, he was known as one of the most beloved of all the presidents up to that point. He was even loved by those who were not Republican. He was the president who made the US a world power. There is a monument dedicated to him in Maryland, two monuments in Ohio— his home state—as well as a statue, and seven schools were named after him. There was also at one point a mountain named after him, which was located in Alaska and was the tallest point in the US. Barack Obama had the mountain renamed Denali.

Besides those who celebrate him and his accomplishments in Ohio, most people today do not know who he is or what he accomplished, which is a shame. Most do not understand how significant his presidency was to the US. McKinley was the last president to serve in the Civil War, and he ran what was referred to as a front porch campaign. This means that while he was running for the presidency, he rarely campaigned outside of his hometown.

McKinley was the first president to have a modern presidency. It was during his presidency that the US's political power expanded globally. He also created amazing economic policies that protected the American industries and allowed them to take root.

If he had not been assassinated, he most likely would have been more remembered than he is today. When the assassination happened, the nation went into deep mourning, just as they did when JFK was assassinated.

It was September 6th of 1901, when a 28-year-old anarchist shot McKinley in the stomach in Buffalo, New York. Emergency surgery was performed, and while things seemed to be going well afterward, the president's health quickly declined. It turned out that gangrene had set in, and the president had developed blood poisoning. He died only eight days after being shot and was the third president to die at the hands of an assassin.

While Roosevelt would eventually overshadow all that McKinley had accomplished, the entire nation mourned his death. King Edward VII declared a time of mourning in honor of McKinley. Cities completely stopped as the train carrying his body passed through on the way to Canton, Ohio. The only other time in history that such mourning was felt for a president was after the assassination of JFK.

President Theodore Roosevelt

Teddy Roosevelt was the toughest president ever. He served two terms and was a strong military commander, a conservationist, and a remarkable adventurer.

In 1883, Teddy headed west for a bit of rest and relaxation after losing the nomination for the Minority Speaker of the House. He arrived in Medora, North Dakota, where he built a log cabin which he planned on using as a retreat.

One evening he was in Mingasville, which was a nearby town, enjoying a drink at the local saloon. A cowboy fired his gun at Teddy several times before pointing it in his face and calling him four eyes. Then, the cowboy told Teddy that he had to buy everyone in the saloon a round of drinks. Teddy was not intimidated though. He laughed in the cowboy's face, charged at him, and then beat him. The cowboy fired again but missed Teddy, who then beat the cowboy's head against the bar until he was no longer conscious. Afterwards, he dragged the cowboy to a shed and locked him in it.

Teddy was an amazingly tough man. He was very popular when he was president, however, not everyone approved of him. Teddy ran against William Howard Taft in 1912, and on October 14th of that year, he was to give a speech in Milwaukee. As he approached the podium, John Schrank, a local saloon keeper, walked up to Teddy and shot him in the chest.

This should have been a fatal blow, but in the pocket of Teddy's shirt was his crumpled speech. The paper protected Teddy. The bullet did not enter his body but instead caused nothing more than a flesh wound. There were fragments of the bullet in his skin, but instead of having them removed, he walked onto the stage, pulled the bloodstained speech out of his pocket and said, "You see, it takes more than a bullet to kill a Bull Moose."

Teddy proceeded with the speech, which lasted an hour. He was woozy as he stepped off the stage and was taken to the hospital where the gunshot wound was treated. While Teddy did not win the election, the incident ensured that he was remembered as the toughest president to have ever served.

President William Taft

William Taft was not only a political heavyweight, but he also tipped the scales at 350 pounds. He was the only president to serve as Supreme Court Chief Justice, and it is said that he got stuck in the bathtub in the White House. The truth is, the story is completely untrue. There is no evidence to base the claim on. However, while he was living in the White House, a new bathtub was installed that ensured he could never get stuck in it.

It was requested that a bathtub big enough to hold the largest man to ever serve as president be brought to the White House. Because there were no tubs that large in Manhattan at the time, it had to be brought through the Panama Canal on a warship.

The tub was seven feet in length, 41 inches wide, and it weighed one ton. The tub was large enough for four average-sized men to sit in comfortably.

It is reported that tubs of this size were not only installed in the White House but on the presidential yacht, as well as in Taft's brother's home in Texas.

The tub was said to be so deep that a normal-sized man would be able to float in it when it was filled with water. After

Taft left the White House, his bathing habits were once again in the news. It is said that while he was staying in a seaside hotel, he did not think about the size of the tub. After filling the tub up, he got in, which caused the tub to overflow. The water then dripped down into the dining room onto the heads of other guests. The next morning as he stared out at the Atlantic Ocean, he said that one day he was going to have a piece of it fenced in, and then he wouldn't have to worry about 'overflowing'.

President Warren Harding

Warren Harding was plagued by presidential scandal which almost made him one of the forgettable presidents. Harding was known as a womanizer, and he had a terrible reputation after he became president—a reputation that was so bad that many historians believe he was one of the worst leaders ever.

The truth is, during his presidency, people loved him. But after he died and word got out about his infidelity, the nation turned on him. Putting his sex life aside, Harding was a very good president.

He worked hard to stabilize the nation after the end of the war. Most nations were left dealing with chaos, but the US just continued on. He pulled our nation out of the Depression after the war and created the first federal budget. He dealt with the racial tensions that had been stirred due to the war, mostly because there had been an influx of African immigrants looking to work in the factories in the north. He was responsible for ending the war with Germany and its allies.

He freed hundreds of political prisoners, ensuring that everyone had the right to the freedom of speech, even if they were speaking out against something the government was doing. And then he had an affair. The woman was thirty years younger than he was. She was in her early 20s, and she did not say anything about the affair until four years after his death, making sure that she completely ruined his reputation.

She wrote a book that was called "The President's Daughter," and it was sold door to door. It discussed the sexual encounters between the two and at the time was considered pornographic. Britton, much to her amazement, was labeled as a degenerate as well as a sexual pervert.

Afterwards, Harding ended up being blamed for scandals he was not even involved in. There was no proof of him being involved in them, however, he was an easy target.

Britton stated that she had no choice but to publish the book. She said that she had pleaded with Harding's family, as well as his supporters, to help care for the child that she bore, but everyone thought of her as nothing more than a gold digger.

It was in 1964 that Harding's letters to a different mistress grabbed the attention of the nation. This woman's name was Carrie Phillips. When you compare the letters written to Phillips to the letters that were written to Britton, you cannot deny that they do sound as if the same man wrote them.

Now, Harding is remembered as a terrible president, a womanizer, and a lazy good for nothing senator, although when you look at what he did accomplish, it is obvious that none of those things is true.

President Calvin Coolidge

Born on the 4th of July, Calvin Coolidge was the 30th President of the US. It was at the 1924 World Series that he threw out the first pitch, and he is well-known for being a civil rights pioneer.

Coolidge lived in a time much like today. Race riots were happening all over the nation; however, at that time it was because for the first time in history, a black man had been nominated as a candidate by the Republican Party for a seat in congress. Many people did not approve of this, but Coolidge had no use for bigotry.

He even faced impeachment when he was governor for standing against the KKK. However, he refused to give up. In one of his letters, he wrote that a man of color deserved just as much of a right to be a candidate as any other citizen of the United States. He said that he refused to shut the door of hope on any man, especially if people expected him to do so based only on the man's race.

President Woodrow Wilson

During his presidency Woodrow Wilson found himself speaking to the American people, trying to convince them that they should stay neutral in the war that was taking place all over the world. It was during this war that he suffered from cerebral thrombosis, which left him not only physically crippled but mentally as well.

Edith, who was his wife, forced the doctor to lie, and she told the nation that according to the nation's top neurologist, the best thing for Wilson was for him to continue on with his presidency. It would take 60 years for the facts to surface, the doctor's notes actually showing that if Wilson was to recover at all, it would be minimal.

In order to keep up her lie, Edith Wilson invited a reporter from The New York World to interview Wilson. During this interview, she lied to him about everything that the president was dealing with. The reporter took notice of his short attention span, his inability to sign his own name, and the fact that his entire left side was paralyze; however, he published exactly what Edith wanted him to. As time went on, the truth began leaking out, and the people of the nation lost faith in the president.

In the following election, the candidates of the Democratic Party tried to follow Wilson's lead, which caused them to lose. Looking back on this almost 100 years later, we have to ask ourselves, what would happen if something like this took place in our White House today? We also have to wonder who was taking care of the presidential duties while Wilson was unable to. Was it Edith? Would doing so technically make her our first female president even if she was not elected by the people?

RANDOM FUN FACTS

1. William Taft was the last President to have facial hair.
2. Teddy Roosevelt had severe asthma when he was growing up and since there were no medications nor inhalers, he was often very ill. Teddy was determined to overcome his illness and did so by exercising regularly. He did suffer from asthma attacks occasionally, but he was no longer ill from them.
3. Woodrow Wilson had dyslexia and struggled his entire life when he was trying to read and even earned his Ph.D.
4. William McKinley was the first candidate for the presidency to use a telephone for the purpose of campaigning.
5. William Taft was the only president to ever swear in two other presidents, Herbert Hoover and Calvin Coolidge.
6. Woodrow Wilson was the highest educated president in the history of the US. He not only had a PhD, but he also had a degree in Political Science as well as one in History. Even though he did not finish law school, he passed the bar exam.
7. It was rumored that Warren Harding was killed by his wife after he had suffered from severe indigestion,

cramps, shortness of breath, and a fever. The president believed that he had food poisoning and died in his office a bit over a week later. She did not kill him, however. Instead, it is likely that he died from a nervous condition as well as congestive heart failure.

8. Each morning while Calvin Coolidge ate his breakfast in bed, he would have someone rub Vaseline on his head.
9. Calvin Coolidge signed the Immigration Act of 1924.
10. Teddy Roosevelt married his fifth cousin once removed and was also related to eleven previous presidents.
11. McKinley was the first president to ever ride in an automobile during his presidency.
12. Grover Cleveland's birth name was Stephen Grover.
13. Although he was not the heaviest president, Grover Cleveland did suffer from obesity and weighed 250 pounds.
14. Benjamin Harrison's supporters gave booze away in order to get votes during his campaign.

TEST YOURSELF- QUESTIONS AND ANSWERS

1. What President's nickname was Big Lub?

   A) William Taft

   B) Woodrow Wilson

   C) William McKinley

2. Who was the first President to have a PhD?

   A) Teddy Roosevelt

   B) Woodrow Wilson

   C) Warren Harding

3. Which President lost the White House china collection, betting it all on one hand in a poker game?

   A) Calvin Coolidge

   B) William Taft

   C) Warren Harding

4. What President was afraid of electricity?

   A) William McKinley

   B) Benjamin Harrison

   C) Grover Cleveland

5. Which President owned over 80 pairs of pants and would take strolls with his friends until 4 a.m.?

   A) Chester Arthur
   B) Woodrow Wilson
   C) Grover Cleveland

ANSWERS

1. A

2. B

3. C

4. B

5. A

CHAPTER FOUR
DEPRESSION

The stock market crashed in 1929, and the Great Depression started. It would last until 1941, hitting the United States hard. The US government took extreme action in order to stimulate the economy, however, this did not work. It would be World War II that would finally bring an end to the Great Depression thanks to the increased need for production.

President Herbert Hoover

Herbert Hoover was known for his offsetting qualities and is considered one of the top ten worst presidents in history. Hoover was elected president just before the Great Depression, and the only skills that he had were that of a manager.

Hoover grew up in Iowa and studied engineering at Stanford. Once the Depression began, he worked to lower taxes and to create new jobs, but he refused to provide any relief for the American people.

This was not his biggest failing. Instead, people saw him as a man who did not know how to communicate well, who was mean-spirited and even uncaring. The homeless even called their makeshift towns Hoovervilles.

The worst thing he is remembered for is signing the Tariff Act into law, which only added fuel to the international trade wars making the Depression worse. It is no wonder that he lost the election to FDR. Even if he had not signed the act, people did not like the way he ran the nation. It is safe to say that Hoover failed to lead the nation in the way that it needed to be led during his presidency.

President Franklin D. Roosevelt

On September 23, 1944, FDR was enjoying a campaign dinner when he made a reference to Fala, his little dog, who had been attacked politically. Roosevelt felt the need to not only defend his reputation but the honor of his little dog as well.

It was rumored that after FDR had visited the Aleutian Island, he left his little dog behind. He was also accused of sending a Navy destroyer back to get Fala, which was rumored to have cost the taxpayers 20 million dollars.

Roosevelt stated that this was completely false and that it was an attempt to stop him from winning the upcoming election. People had used his dog as a way to attack him. FDR stated that other political parties were trying to distract the American people from more important issues by attacking his defenseless dog.

Fala was a black Scottish terrier, and she went almost everywhere with FDR. He was very fond of her. She could be seen in the Oval Office while he worked, and she was even taken to meet Winston Churchill at one point.

Eleanor did not approve of a dog being in the White House, but FDR was not going to let her leave his side. She slept at the foot of FDR's bed, he was the only person that was allowed to feed her, and each morning when the President was brought his breakfast, Fala was brought a bone.

Fala continued to live with Eleanor after FDR died and passed when she was 12 years old. She was buried in Hyde Park, New York, near the man who was so attached to her during his life.

President Harry Truman

During his campaign, Truman focused on civil rights. He knew that it was the right thing for him to do, but he also felt that if he wanted to win the election, he had to win the black vote.

At that time, all the public polls showed that the Republican candidate would win by a landslide. Truman, however, thought that it would be the black vote that would determine who would be the next president.

It was that election that would result in what is known as the greatest presidential election upset in history. Almost every prediction indicated that Thomas Dewey was going to be the next president, but Truman won, amazingly overcoming a three-way split in the Democratic Party and receiving 303 electoral votes. He also won the popular vote.

While the election was a complete surprise, it was the fifth win in a row for the party. It was during this election that the Democrats not only took control of the White House but the Senate and the House of Representatives as well. It was this election that proved the Democratic Party was the majority party at that point. It would remain this way until 1952.

Truman ratified the 22nd Amendment, which limited the president to serving two terms. During this election, Truman won Tennessee; however, one elector went rogue and cast their vote for Thurmond.

President Dwight Eisenhower

It was on June 5, 1944, when Eisenhower gave his speech to the United States soldiers just one day before they were to invade Normandy. The following day, General Dwight D. Eisenhower would lead the Allied Expeditionary Forces as they stormed the shores of Normandy. It was this day that was the beginning of the end of World War II.

There were around 156,000 soldiers, no less than 4,000 ships, and 11,000 planes that invaded Europe that day. At the time, it was called Operation Overlord. Today, we know it as D-Day.

D-Day weighed heavy on Eisenhower. He was not just nervous, he was tense, and he worked to plan every action nonstop for months. He knew that all of it rested on his shoulders. It is said that he lived off of cigarettes and coffee, he smoked up to four packs a day, and he had dangerously high blood pressure.

After addressing the soldiers, Eisenhower returned to his trailer and wrote a note. It stated that he had imagined that the landing failed. He said that he did not imagine it was due to the troops under his command but instead was his own fault.

The man had spent months thinking of everything that could have gone wrong. He had to put his faith in the troops, as well as the commanders, to carry out the plan he had created. However, he refused to blame them if it failed.

He had even considered postponing the operation for 24 hours because the weather was bad. However, he knew that it was impossible to keep an operation like that secret, and since the Germans knew that the American soldiers were on their way, he only had a three-day window.

As he gave the speech to the soldiers, we can only imagine what was going through his mind. He did his best to encourage them, to put them in the right frame of mind in order to ensure their success, and he had to know that a lot of the young men that he was sending to war would not be returning home.

He spoke about how those men would be burdened for the rest of their lives by having to take the lives of others. The soldiers knew that they were going into war, but they were cocky as young men are and did not think anything could happen to them.

Today, we know what those soldiers were headed into, but back then, they and the rest of America were completely ignorant of what Hitler's regime was actually doing. We cannot imagine what went through those young men's minds as they stormed that beach, but I imagine they heard the voice of their general telling them he would accept nothing less than victory.

President John F. Kennedy

It was November 22, 1963, at 12:30 p.m. when time stood still in the United States of America. That was when Lee Harvey Oswald fired three shots from the Texas School Book Depository Building. Governor Connally was wounded, and John Fitzgerald Kennedy, the people's president, was fatally wounded.

JFK and Jackie Kennedy had been traveling in a 10-mile motorcade in downtown Dallas, Texas. The couple rode in a Lincoln convertible waving at the crowd that stood along the sides of the road hoping to get a glimpse of the President and First Lady. As the bullet hit JFK, Jackie grabbed her husband's head, and the nation went into shock. It was a time that would never be forgotten by those who witnessed it. Everyone who was alive at the time still knows exactly where they were and what they were doing when they heard that the president had been assassinated.

Lyndon Johnson was traveling just three cars behind the president and witnessed the entire thing. He would be sworn in as president just two hours after the shots were fired. Jackie was one of the thirty people who witnessed the swearing in. She was still wearing the clothes that were covered in JFK's blood.

The following day, it was announced that the 25th of November would be declared a national day of mourning for JFK. The day of his funeral, hundreds of thousands stood on the streets in DC, watching the horse-drawn caisson that carried the body of JFK to St. Matthew's Cathedral. Afterwards, it continued to Arlington National Cemetery.

The leaders of 99 nations gathered at the funeral. JFK was buried below Arlington House, where an eternal flame still burns.

Oswald grew up in New Orleans and was born in 1939. In 1956, he joined the Marines, but he was discharged three years later. Nine years after being discharged, he traveled to the Soviet Union where he tried and failed to become a citizen. He returned to the US in 1962 with his wife, who was a Soviet woman, and their baby daughter.

In 1963, he ordered a .38 revolver and a rifle with a telescope by mail order. On the 10th of April, he tried to shoot Edwin Walker, a former general in the US Army. Later in the month, he would return to New Orleans to found a pro-Castro organization called the Fair Play for Cuba Committee.

In September, he traveled to Mexico City, where he tried to get a visa so that he could travel to Cuba. Then, in October, he began working at the Texas School Book Depository Building where from a sixth-floor window, he would assassinate the 35th President of the United States.

It was less than one hour after he shot JFK that he killed a police officer who was questioning him in the street. Just thirty minutes after that shooting, the police received a call reporting that he was in a movie theater, and he was arrested.

It was on the 24th of November during a press conference that Jack Ruby would shoot Oswald with a .38 revolver, killing him. Some called Ruby a hero; however, he had killed a man and was charged with murder. According to conspiracy theorists, Ruby killed Oswald in order to cover up a large conspiracy that led back to the FBI.

Ruby never faced trial. It was found that he could not get a fair trial in Texas, and while he was awaiting trial, he died of lung cancer.

President Lyndon B. Johnson

Johnson is known for his huge ego as well as his... Johnson. He believed that his was the largest ever, and he was not shy about letting people know. He had a love affair with his penis and loved to tell stories about it.

His obsession with his penis began when he was in college. He had no problem exposing himself to his roommates or coming home after a date and telling them that "Jumbo," as he dubbed it, had a real workout. It is said that he would then go into great detail about his intimate relations.

When LBJ was asked to explain the Vietnam war to reporters in an off-the-record moment, one of the reporters simply asked him "Why?" LBJ responded by exposing his useless flaccid sword and exclaiming, "That's why."

He had no problem displaying it to his colleagues either. He was known for showing it off. One story says that while in the bathroom, he 'helicoptered' his penis, asking one of his colleagues if he had ever seen anything that big. Quite the question coming from the President of the United States. I can't imagine that the man was going to tell the president anything less than what he wanted to hear.

Johnson had no problem urinating whenever or wherever he felt the urge to do so. He had no problem whipping it out and urinating even in the parking lot of the House Office Building. One man said that he and Johnson were walking across a parking lot, there were female secretaries walking behind them, and Johnson just stopped walking and began urinating right in front of the women. He even relieved himself in the corner sink in one of the offices of the House Office Building while he continued to dictate to his secretary.

So obsessed he was with his penis, Johnson had a special showerhead installed in the White House shower that was to be aimed directly at it. The water lines had to be replaced with larger lines because he wanted the showerhead to have so much pressure that it was taking the pressure from the rest of the White House. One of the ushers tried the showerhead, and it is said that he was pinned against the back shower wall the pressure was so strong. It is a wonder that the president was able to withstand such force, especially when pointed at such an um… delicate area.

According to Richard Bolling, who was the Missouri representative, LBJ was constantly pulling on his testicles, not caring whether males or females were present. It was so extreme that even men were embarrassed by it.

His love for his penis was not kept private at all. He was well known for displaying his affection for his penis in public, even when he was on the floor of the Senate or House. He would reach his hand into his pocket and lift his leg, propping his foot on a chair in order to allow himself more access. He also had no problem scratching quite deeply into his buttocks while in public.

He wanted to make sure that his huge penis and testicles were properly accommodated, therefore, he ordered custom pants from Joe Haggar. He told Joe that the crotch was always a little too tight on his testicles (although he did not use that term) and that he needed an extra inch because regular pants felt like he was riding a barbed wire fence.

While LBJ's obsession with his Johnson has nothing to do with anything he accomplished during his presidency, it is one of the things he is most remembered for.

President Richard Nixon

Many people cannot help but see the similarities between Richard Nixon and Donald J. Trump. First, neither of them look like other presidents. Nixon had low jowls, unlike the dignified presidents of the past. But the thing that stands out the most is that Nixon had—just as Trump currently has—a very strong dislike for the media.

Nixon knew that the media was his enemy. He would often tell his aides to write it out 100 times and to make sure that they never forgot it. Nixon also believed that Johnson had wiretapped him. J. Edgar Hoover was said to be the one who tipped him off about the wiretap.

Nixon, however, was involved in Watergate. The scandal began on the 17th of June 1972 with the arrest of several burglars who were discovered in the Democratic National Committee located in the Watergate complex.

Of course, this was not an ordinary robbery. As it turned out, these burglars were connected to the president's reelection campaign. They were stealing documents and putting wiretaps on the phones.

Richard Nixon worked very hard to cover up the crime, but in August 1974, it was discovered that he had played a role, and this resulted in his resignation. It was this scandal that would lead the American people to start questioning their potential presidents and to think more about who they were voting for.

The illegal espionage at the time seemed critical to the president and his advisors. The group had already put taps on the phones, but they had not worked. Therefore, five men returned in order to put a new microphone in the office and steal top secret documents. The security guards working at the time noticed that there was tape placed over several of the locks on the doors of the building.

The guards called the police, and the men were caught in the building. It was not clear right away that the men were connected with the president, but when copies of the reelection committee's White House telephone number were found mixed in with the belongings of the burglars, suspicions were raised.

In August, Nixon told the nation that no one at the White House had been involved, and most of the voters believed him. He was reelected in November 1972, winning by a landslide.

Later, it was found that Nixon had not been telling the truth. Just days after the arrest, Nixon had provided the burglars with hundreds of thousands of dollars in what is believed to be hush money. The president and his aides also tried to force the CIA to impede the investigation that was being conducted by the FBI. This crime was even more serious than the original.

While all of this was going on, seven people faced charges which were related to Watergate. Five of them pled guilty, and the other two were later convicted of the crime.

It was not until the following year that Nixon resigned and Gerald Ford was sworn in as the President of the United

States. Ford then pardoned Nixon for his crimes. However, not all of his aides were so lucky and instead they ended up in federal prison.

Nixon abused the power that came with the position of President of the United States and brought distrust to the office. Americans were already dealing with the outcome of the Vietnam War, the assassinations of Martin Luther King Jr. and Robert Kennedy, as well as other national leaders. The Watergate scandal left the people of the nation feeling sour.

President Gerald Ford

Gerald Ford, while not given credit for it, was a very funny man. You see, once while he was getting off of Air Force One, he stumbled, and that seemed to be the moment in his career that people remembered him by. They believed that Ford was a clumsy man, and some even believed that he was not very smart.

LBJ had even stated that Ford was not able to walk and chew gum at the same time. Ford, however, graduated from Yale Law School, which is one of the hardest schools in the US to get into. Nevertheless, people continued to believe the inaccuracies that were spread about him.

Somehow, while we give Reagan credit for being a funny president, and we know that LBJ was more mean and sarcastic than he was funny, Ford has been thrown into the same category with Nixon and Carter, clueless when it came to humor.

This simply was not true. Once when a person tried to give Ford a telephone that looked like a lamp, he kindly declined, stating that his image had enough problems without him having to excuse himself to answer his lamp.

Ford was also probably the most athletic president to ever live in the White House, but he had no problem making fun of his own abilities. He once stated that Betty had told him he was a terrible dancer and that the only reason he played center in football was because he didn't have to worry about moving his feet.

Many people believe that Reagan was a master of storytelling and timing, and while he was great, so was Ford. Ford had the ability to tell the short, medium, and long version of any story. When he told the story about the year he played the center on Michigan's football team, if he was telling the short story, it was simply that they lost seven of the eight games they played.

When he told the long version, he would go through each game. However, whether the short or the long version was being told, the punch line remained the same. He would pause after the story and then state that what really hurt him that year (after losing all but one game) was that he was named MVP. It was a story that was sure to get a laugh by all that heard it.

He loved to play golf and often told a story about the time that he ran into Jack Nichols, Ben Hogan, and Byron Nelson at a club before they teed off. He would always say that he walked up to them expecting that they would ask him to join them. They would tell him that they needed a fourth player that could keep up with them. Ford said that he told them, "Well, here I am!" He said that they said it was good and that he could help them look for their fourth.

Former President Gerald Ford even wrote "Humor and the Presidency," a book about humor. It is a great read and a great way to see how he used humor as well as why it is important for a president to use humor. Ford wrote that there were two ways to experience humor. You could be the perpetrator or the victim, and as the victim of humor, he had not taken a backseat to anyone.

He was a great man who did not let what people said about him bother him. In fact, when people spoke of him and made fun of him or talked about how clumsy or dumb he was, his wife Betty said it all rolled off of his back because he had such a great sense of humor.

President Jimmy Carter

Jimmy Carter's brother took some money from the family business while he was living on the family's peanut farm, which resulted in Carter and his family being investigated for six months by a special prosecutor. It was the job of that prosecutor to go through every peanut shell on the farm in order to dig up any scandalous information about the Carter family or the farm.

What really happened was that Billy was paid around 20,000 dollars per year, but year after year, he decided that he was going to help himself to the rest of the money made by the farm.

He took money from the family business each year until it started to attract the attention of Congress. Congress was sure that the president was using the money as a political slush fund because they did not know at the time that it was his brother Billy taking it.

Of course, it turned out that his brother—who was not the best employee—was taking money from the family farm. Not exactly the scandal that everyone had been looking for, but the investigation did lead to Carter losing the farm.

RANDOM FUN FACTS

1. Before Hoover became President, he lived in China where he learned how to speak Mandarin Chinese. He and his wife were known for speaking Mandarin Chinese when they were in the White House so that other people would not be able to understand what they were saying to each other.
2. In the credits of the movie "The President's Mystery," Franklin D. Roosevelt received the Story By credit.
3. FDR served longer than any other president, serving more than twelve years in the White House. It was his presidency that caused momentum to grow for the 22nd amendment, which stated that no president could serve more than two terms.
4. Before Harry Truman became the President of the US, he was a man's outfitter, but his business went bankrupt.
5. The American people were not upset during the 1948 Election Upset even though the media swore that Truman was going to lose to Dewey, at least according to the public polls. It seemed that members of the media were the only ones who were upset after the election.
6. When Eisenhower was in his freshman year in high

school, he suffered a knee injury which resulted in such a severe infection that the doctors thought he would die. The doctors wanted to remove his leg; however, the boy refused because he loved to play sports. It is unknown how he recovered so miraculously.

7. JFK's father, who was a Harvard alum, wrote JFK a letter of recommendation which stated that JFK was careless and that he lacked application. Not a very glowing recommendation. On top of that, JFK did not have a very impressive application.
8. John F. Kennedy had struggled with his health his entire life and fearing death, he had his last rites given to him three times before he became the president.
9. In 1964, Johnson declared the war on poverty.
10. The Vietnam War caused Johnson to suffer from depression, which brought his presidency to an end.
11. Johnson would regularly request that the staff of the White House follow him into the bathroom so that he could continue their conversation while relieving himself.
12. While Richard Nixon was serving in the Navy, he saw that people were winning money by playing poker. Nixon was an opportunist and had the best player in the unit teach him how to play poker. Within a matter of months, he had won over six thousand dollars, which he would

later use toward his first congressional campaign.

13. Before Gerald Ford became president, he and his wife were fashion models. His wife was also a dancer and had used the money she earned from modeling to put herself through dance school.

14. Before Jimmy Carter was the president, he owned a peanut farm. When he was inaugurated, a large balloon in the shape of a peanut was part of the parade. It was a bit of tribute to his family's peanut farm.

15. Ronald Reagan was an actor before he became President of the United States. When his acting career was not going well, he did standup comedy.

TEST YOURSELF – QUESTIONS AND ANSWERS

1. Which President was enlisted in the National Guard and served as an artillery commander during the first World War?

   A) FDR
   B) Harry Truman
   C) Lyndon B. Johnson

2. Who was the first president to ever ride in a helicopter?

   A) Eisenhower
   B) Richard Nixon
   C) Gerald Ford

3. What President dropped the atomic bombs on Nagasaki and Hiroshima?

   A) Jimmy Carter
   B) Lyndon B. Johnson
   C) John F. Kennedy

4. What president said, "Those who make peaceful revolution impossible make violent revolution inevitable?"

   A) Dwight Eisenhower

B) Richard Nixon

C) John F. Kennedy

5. For which president's grandson is Camp David named?

A) Harry Truman

B) Dwight Eisenhower

C) Franklin D. Roosevelt

ANSWERS

1. B

2. A

3. B

4. C

5. B

CHAPTER FIVE

PEACE THROUGH STRENGTH ABROAD

The confidence of the American people in the nation was restored. There was progress, there was growth, and Americans were optimistic. It began with Reagan, and even today it continues on.

President Ronald Reagan

Reagan was an amazing president. He was the president during the last innocent time in the US. He was determined to reduce the American people's dependence on the government. He was not a politician, but instead, he was an actor who was in 53 films.

He was married to Jane Wyman. The couple had two children, Michael and Maureen. Then, in 1952, he married Nancy Davis, who was an actress. The couple had Patricia Ann and Ronald Prescott.

While working in the film industry, his views switched from Democrat to Republican. He then became a spokesman for the Republican beliefs. He was elected the governor of California in 1966 and then reelected in 1970. In 1980, he won the Republican nomination for president and choose George Bush as his running mate. Ronald Reagan won with 489 electoral votes; Carter only received 49.

Sixty-nine days after taking office, he was shot by his would-be assassin. However, Reagan quickly recovered and was back to work.

In Today's modern politics, there are some pretty interesting similarities between President Trump and Reagan. Trump, like Reagan, is a Washington outsider. They were both dismissed as serious candidates, and both were attacked and said to be extremists as well as simplistic. They both share the same views on illegal immigration. Trump was also a Democrat before he became a Republican. Both were TV stars. Trump has actually stated that he wants to follow in Reagan's footsteps.

Both of them succeeded a liberal president who was focused on big government. Both are opposed to the union, and both wanted to Make America Great Again, which was Reagan's slogan that could be found on campaign material.

Reagan will always be remembered as the president that Made America Great Again. By increasing defense spending by 35 percent, he made the military strong, but he also helped to improve the United States' relationship with the Soviet Union.

President George H.W. Bush

George H.W. Bush was born on the 12th of June in 1924. He served in WWII and in the House of Representatives. He also served as the Vice President of the United States for two terms while Reagan was president. Bush won the election in 1988; however, when he ran for his second term, he lost to Bill Clinton.

When Bush turned 18 years old, he enlisted in the Navy and became the youngest Navy pilot to serve in WWII. He was a combat pilot during the war and flew his torpedo bomber on 58 missions. His plane was once hit over the Pacific, and he narrowly averted death.

He was the first sitting vice president to win an election since 1837 and was known for the saying, "Read my lips—no new taxes."

While he was president, he helped to dissolve the Soviet Union, and he responded to Saddam Hussein's invasion of Kuwait. He tried to use a military strike to drive the dictator out of Kuwait, and the mission was viewed as a success.

President Bill Clinton

"I did not have sex with that woman," is probably one of the most memorable things Bill Clinton ever said. However, many people do not know that this was not the only scandal that the Clintons were involved in. In fact, a cloud of scandal surrounds them, more than any other first family before them.

It began with Travelgate, Watergate, Filegate, the removal of Vince Foster's office, the Rose Law Firm billing records that disappeared, the selling of the seats on the Commerce Department of International Trade Missions, the renting out of the Lincoln bedroom and using the funds as campaign contributions, the Charlie Trie scandal, the Johnny Chung scandal, the Monica Lewinsky scandal, the impeachment, Pardongate, the Bosnia airport sniper lie, Benghazi, the email scandal, and the Clinton Foundation scandal.

Of course, not all of these scandals took place while Bill was in office; however, when looking back, they will taint his legacy, if they have not already.

Bill Clinton was the second president to ever be impeached by the House of Representatives, although they did not force him to leave the office. He was found guilty of obstructing justice, as well as of perjury. He had been under investigation for having a sexual relationship with a White House intern named Monica Lewinsky. Hillary, blamed the right, saying that it was a conspiracy against Bill that had started the day that he had won the election.

President George W. Bush

The son of former President George H.W. Bush was a very likable president. He made the American people laugh as he jumbled his words, but he also led the nation through one of the most heartbreaking times in history.

A few of Bush's blunders include:

"Rarely is the question asked, is our children learning?"

"They have misunderestimated me."

"He married a Texas girl, a West Texas girl, just like me."

"I know the human being and the fish can coexist peacefully."

"George Washington was the first president. Of course, the most interesting thing about him is that I read three or four books about him last year. Isn't that interesting?"

"A low voter turnout is an indication that fewer people are going to the polls."

With all of the anger surrounding politics today, it is great to take a few minutes and remember the funny moments that George Bush gave us. He is a man who does not care what people think, one that is himself, and loves who he is. He is also one who is loved by the people.

President Barack Obama

The legacy of Obama is unusually complex. Obama was the first African-American president, which showed that the nation had moved past its hostility toward blacks. He was president during the Great Recession, and Osama bin Laden was killed during his presidency.

President Obama will always be remembered for his charisma and character and skilled dance moves that he showed off at The Ellen DeGeneres Show. Here are some more interesting facts about Barack Obama.

- The name Barack means "one who is blessed" in Swahili.
- He was known as "O'Bomber" at high school for his skill at basketball.
- He is left-handed – the sixth post-war president to be left-handed.
- Obama once said the three men he admired the most were Mahatma Gandhi, Abraham Lincoln, and Martin Luther King, Jr.
- 71 years after Hiroshima bombing, Barack Obama was USA's first sitting President to visit the place.
- He addresses David Cameron – Prime Minister of the UK as 'Bro'.

RANDOM FUN FACTS

1. Barack Obama collects Conan the Barbarian and Spiderman comic books. He has also read all of the Harry Potter books.

2. George H.W. Bush was a very athletic man when he was in high school. He had been the captain of not only the varsity soccer team but the baseball team as well. On top of that, he played on the basketball team.

3. Bill Clinton did eventually admit that he had an inappropriate relationship with Monica Lewinsky.

4. George W. Bush was the head cheerleader when he was in high school and spent his time organizing pep talks as well as skits that were performed at the school's assemblies.

5. Donald J. Trump has never smoked a cigarette, never drank alcohol, nor has he done any drugs. His brother Fred suffered from alcoholism for years which resulted in his death, but before he died, he warned Trump of the dangers of drinking.

TEST YOURSELF – QUESTIONS AND ANSWERS

1. What president and his wife were involved in the Whitewater scandal?

   A) Ronald Reagan
   B) George Bush Sr.
   C) Bill Clinton

2. Which president is known for his funky sock collection?

   A) Barack Obama
   B) George Bush Sr.
   C) Donald Trump

3. What president was called 'Bubba' while he was growing up?

   A) Donald Trump
   B) George W. Bush
   C) Bill Clinton

4. Which president has a star on the Hollywood Walk of Fame? It was the 2327th star to be added to the Walk of Fame?

   A) Bill Clinton
   B) Donald Trump
   C) Barack Obama

5. Who insulted Ronald Reagan in his book "The Art of the Deal," which was published in 1987?

   A) Donald Trump
   B) Barack Obama
   C) George W Bush

ANSWERS

6. C
7. B
8. C
9. B
10. A

DON'T FORGET YOUR FREE BOOKS

GET THEM FOR FREE ON

WWW.TRIVIABILL.COM

MORE BOOKS BY BILL O'NEILL

I hope you enjoyed this book and learned something new. Please feel free to check out some of my previous books on **Amazon**.

IF YOU LIKED THIS BOOK, I WOULD REALLY APPRECIATE IF YOU COULD LEAVE A SHORT LITTLE REVIEW ON AMAZON BY CLICKING HERE

Made in the USA
Middletown, DE
17 December 2024